"Gripping and compelling...With new evi P9-APM-305 Fetzer and Jacobs systematically appraise the alternative explanations for the death of a United States Senator. Their conclusion—that Paul Wellstone was the target of an assassination—is very disturbing. It should motivate local authorities to launch a formal inquiry into the death of this remarkable American."

—Donald T. Phillips
Author, *Lincoln on Leadership*

"A TREMENDOUS COLLABORATION IN COURAGE"

"Meticulous research...rigorous analysis. Their efforts lead us to only one conclusion...much of the circumstantial evidence incriminates Vice-President Dick Cheney and other prominent figures in the Bush Administration as having some involvement in Wellstone's death."

"This book represents a tremendous collaboration in courage. In chronicling yet another chapter in what has rapidly become one the darkest eras in the history of American democracy, this book deserves far more serious attention than it will likely receive from the mainstream of American journalism and scholarship."

—David Gabbard
Professor, East Carolina University
Author, *Knowledge and Power in the Global Economy*

ADVANCE PRAISE FOR AMERICAN ASSASSINATION

"By unraveling the conditions under which he died, Four Arrows and Jim Fetzer have not only paid tribute to Paul Wellstone, they've brought to light the facts surrounding yet another suspicious plane crash in a lineage that extends back to Governor Mel Carnahan, Senator John Tower, and Congressman Hale Boggs."

—Russ Wellen
Freezerbox.com

AMERICAN ASSASSINATION

THE STRANGE DEATH OF SENATOR PAUL WELLSTONE

BY FOUR ARROWS
(AKA DON TRENT JACOBS, PH.D., ED.D.)

&

JAMES H. FETZER, PH.D.

American Assassination:
The Strange Death of Senator Paul Wellstone

©2004 Don Trent Jacobs
and James H. Fetzer

First Edition, First Printing
Printed on 50% Recycled Paper
at Thomson-Shore, Dexter, MI
An Employee-Owned Company

Vox Pop #1
Edited by Sander Hicks
Published October, 2004
ISBN: 0-9752763-0-1

Vox Pop
is a Project of the
Drench Kiss Media Corporation

Vox Pop/DKMC
1022 Cortelyou Road
Brooklyn, NY 11218-5302

www.drenchkiss.com

Paul David Wellstone
in memoriam

Four Arrows: *Why was the FBI not listed as party to the investigation in the final NTSB report on the Wellstone case?*

Frank Hilldrup at NTSB: *They were not a party to the investigation.*

FA: *Then what were they doing on the scene for about 8 hours prior to the arrival of the NTSB team?*

FH: *I can't say for sure, since I only took over on Monday; but maybe they were there responding to the—you know—the conspiracy theories.*

FA: *How could there have been any conspiracy theories operating before the plane crashed?*

FH: *Well, uh, of course, that's true. Well, the FBI might have been there to identify the bodies as they sometimes do in airplane accidents. I'm not really sure but there is someone with the FBI I can call who was there. I'll get back to you about this.*

FA: *I'd really appreciate it. Don't you think it strange?*

FH: *Well, I just know everything is above board but I do want to find out.*

FA: *One more question. Why no public hearing for this incident?*

FH: *We only have hearings for high profile cases.*

—phone conversation between Four Arrows (FA) and Frank Hilldrup (FH), the lead investigator for the NTSB (Thursday, 19 February 2004)

CONTENTS

PREFACE

> The one who derives advantage from a crime is the one most likely to
> have committed it.
>
> —Seneca

Before the election of 2002, the United States Senate was divided
50-49 with the Democrats in control. This split had come about as a
result of the decision by Vermont Senator James Jeffords to disavow
his Republican status and declare himself an Independent. Georgia
Senator Max Cleland lost his bid for re-election in a race he had been
widely expected to win, but the votes had been tabulated by
electronic voting machines. The sudden death of Minnesota Senator
Paul Wellstone not only deprived the Democrats of a majority during the lame-duck session after the election, but the subsequent loss
by Walter Mondale to Norm Coleman, whom Wellstone was defeat-
ing, cost them control of the Senate.

At the time, Coleman's victory was hailed as evidence of the power
of the Bush machine, where the President was said to have placed his
reputation "on the line". But in Cleland's case, studies have suggested his loss was due to manipulation of electronic polls. If the death
of Paul Wellstone, who was pulling ahead of Norm Coleman, was no
accident, then it may have been far less of a political risk for George
Bush to have campaigned aggressively for a predetermined result. If
the Republicans proved anything during the fiasco in Florida, it's
that they can count. The outcome was control of the Senate, 51-48,
with one lone Independent.

Although there have been many studies about how electronic
voting machines can be used to steal elections, there are few studies
of the death of this American icon, Senator Paul Wellstone. We have
been inspired by the earlier research of those who have shown the
courage to confront the all too real possibility that democracy was
defeated during the election of 2002 by the use of underhanded
means: theft in Georgia and murder in Minnesota. We are especially
indebted to Michael Niman of Buffalo State College, Christopher

Bollyn of *AmericanFreePress.com*, and Michael Ruppert of *FromTheWilderness.com*.

While taking into account their personal reports and preliminary inquiries, we have undertaken an independent and objective analysis of the available evidence in this case, using the pattern of scientific reasoning known as "inference to the best explanation". We do not simply believe as an article of faith (based on intuition or mere speculation) that Senator Paul Wellstone's death was an assassination rather than an accident. In these pages we have proven beyond reasonable doubt that the official account presented by the National Transportation Safety Board (NTSB) cannot be logically sustained. Its "findings" are even contradicted by its own evidence. We have also proven that the likelihood of an assassination—which is an hypothesis the NTSB did not consider—is greater than the likelihood of an accident. The assassination hypothesis provides a better explanation than the alternative.

This book has been organized into seven chapters, plus a Prologue and an Epilogue. Chapter 1, "Something's Fishy," opens with a critical analysis of early news reports about the weather, the FBI's early arrival, and NTSB observations on the scene, which raise the prospect that a cover-up may have been in the making early-on.

Chapter 2, "Motives for Murder," shows clear motivation. It reveals why certain forces in the current US government, right-wing politicians, and a variety of corporate interests had ample reasons for taking out the Minnesota Senator and discusses early stage in the research that has brought us to the conclusions we have presented here.

Chapter 3, "Gathering Evidence," brings together kinds of evidence that the NTSB did not consider but which make a difference to understanding what happened here. They suggest the official investigation of the Wellstone plane crash was seriously incomplete, at best, and, at worst, possibly corrupt. The term "farce" has been used more than once to describe NTSB investigations in the past. This case illustrates why.

Chapter 4, "Assassination Science," presents an overview of the application of scientific reasoning to analyze the cause of death in other cases that, like this one, are politically explosive. It explores the use of the phrase, "conspiracy theory," as an excuse to dismiss out of hand—without even considering the available relevant evidence—troubling prospects that are "too messy" or too painful to confront.

Chapter 5, "Thinking Things Through," applies scientific reasoning to the investigation of the death of Senator Paul Wellstone, where the earliest accounts of the crash were clearly mistaken, a cover-up appears to have been imposed, and previously neglected alternative explanations are those most likely to be true. Comparisons and contrasts are drawn with other controversial cases, including the death of JFK.

Chapter 6, "The Official Story," focuses intensely upon the NTSB's long-anticipated report on the airplane crash that took the Senator's life. Released after more than a year of study, the official account is not even consistent with the NTSB's own evidence. This chapter explains in detail why it cannot withstand critical scrutiny and deserves to be rejected.

Chapter 7, "How it was Done," advances a vastly more plausible explanation of what actually happened to the Wellstone plane. The analysis is rigorous and thorough, demonstrating that the assassination hypothesis provides a far more adequate account of the evidence. It also implies that—for several dreadful minutes—the passengers aboard had to know that their plane had been sabotaged and that they were doomed.

The Epilogue emphasizes that what we don't know can still hurt us. We are ensnared in the grasp of powerful forces who want to maximize corporate profits regardless of the costs to our democracy. Extricating ourselves from their grip dictates that all of us must understand the threat they pose to the American way of life, which they appear to be intent upon assassinating.

The Appendices, finally, illustrate Senator Paul Wellstone's courageous stands against the rich and powerful with an overview of his "Platform," which was an agenda for improving the life of every American, not just the privileged few. And his outspoken opposition to injustice and inhumanity is exemplified by his speech, "On Iraq," which illustrate his courage, his intelligence, and his integrity.

The loss of Paul Wellstone has made a monumental difference, not simply for the State of Minnesota but for all Americans. The concluding section is no mere appendage, but reflects the core of the issues at stake in this study. When you read this man's own words and recall his commitment to standing up for "the little fellers, not the Rockefellers," you begin to appreciate why there was a very real chance he might have been assassinated. Questions about his death, as painful as they may be, simply can not be ignored as long as *we the people* want to preserve genuine democracy.

PROLOGUE

"Will no one rid me of this turbulent priest?"

—Attributed to King Henry II
before the murder of St. Thomas á Becket

Often called "the conscience of the Senate," *Mother Jones* once described Senator Wellstone as "The first 1960s radical elected to the United States Senate." Wellstone was the Senate's strongest, most persistent, articulate, and outspoken opponent of the administration of George W. Bush. He was frequently the lone voice in opposing status-quo policies of both Republicans and Democrats, and yet, polls showed that his popularity surged after he voted to oppose the Senate resolution authorizing Bush to wage war in Iraq. It is difficult to imagine how high his standing would have become in light of recent history, but there can be no doubt his popularity in Minnesota and across the nation would have been immense.

The death of Senator Wellstone was strange in many ways. Blame for the crash that caused his death was initially cast upon the weather, which was widely misdescribed as involving freezing rain. When the weather turned out to be only moderately difficult, responsibility was directed against the pilots, even though the principal pilot, Richard Conry, had 5,200 hours of experience, the highest possible rating, and had passed his FAA "flight check" just two days before the fatal flight. One former co-pilot, who had accompanied him 50 times, even described him as the most careful pilot with whom he had ever flown. The situation was peculiar.

Early reports suggested that the cause of the crash might never be known. That was very odd, because an investigation had yet to be conducted. A rapid-response team from the St. Paul FBI descended on the scene as early as 12 noon, even though the crash site had only been identified at 11 AM by Gary Ulman, the Eveleth-Virginia Airport Assistant Manger, who had not notified them. Rick Wahlberg, the Sheriff of St. Louis County, arrived on the scene at

1:30 PM and observed the FBI agents there, some of whom he knew personally. Gary Ulman would confirm that they had been there at least since 1 PM. But an FBI spokesman, Paul McCabe, would later maintain that the FBI had actually arrived much later, at 3:30 PM.

Calculations indicated that for the FBI to have arrived by noon, they would have had to have departed from St. Paul around 9:30 AM and flown to Duluth, where they rented cars and traveled the rest of the way to Eveleth-Virginia. These calculations were based upon minimal times for getting to the airport, boarding the plane, getting into the air, and arriving in Duluth. Yet they intractably establish that the FBI had to have departed from St. Paul at approximately the same time the Senator's plane was taking off, displaying remarkable powers of prognostication in anticipating the occurrence of a crash at a scene they would otherwise not have reached for hours.

The following day, acting NTSB Director Carol Carmody, a former employee with the CIA, who was in charge of this inquiry (as she had been of that for Governor Mel Carnahan of Missouri) announced that the FBI had determined that no terrorist activity had been involved in bringing the plane down. This was quite remarkable on several grounds. It was the responsibility of the National Transportation Safety Board (NTSB), not the FBI, to determine the cause of the crash. The NTSB investigation would eventually take more than a year. Anyone who thought twice about the matter had to be puzzled how the FBI could assure the NTSB that no terrorist activity had been involved when the cause of the crash had yet to be determined.

These were only a few of the peculiar circumstances surrounding the death of Paul Wellstone that have struck many as rather strange. In an early article on this case, Michael I. Niman, professor of journalism and of media studies at Buffalo State College, suggested that Wellstone's death might not have been accidental. Boldly asking, "Was Paul Wellstone Murdered?", Niman offered multiple reasons why that might be the case. He began by describing Senator Wellstone, who had been killed along with his activist wife, Sheila, just prior to an election that he was probably going to win, as "the only progressive in the U.S. Senate".

Niman reports—what was common knowledge in Washington, D.C., at the time—that the Bush administration had made

Wellstone's defeat the number one priority of 2002. Observing that Wellstone is not the first American politician to die in a small plane crash, he discusses the strikingly similar death of Missouri's former governor, Mel Carnahan, who lost his life in 2000 three weeks before election day, attempting to unseat incumbent John Ashcroft.

Perhaps we ought to have learned something from its occurrence at the time, but the citizens of Missouri preferred to vote for a dead man to returning Ashcroft to the Senate. Carnahan's wife would be appointed to the seat, while Bush would make Ashcroft Attorney General of the United States.   Another death Niman discusses has its own ironies.

Emphasizing the utility of the airplane as a possible instrument of assassination, Niman remarks on the earlier death of Panamanian General Omar Torrijos, who, after he had thumbed his nose at the Reagan/Bush administration, died when the instruments in his plane failed to function during takeoff. Niman notes that he (Torrijos) would be replaced by Manuel Noriega, a CIA operative who had worked closely with George Herbert Walker Bush, who was its past Director. Some may find Niman's implications disturbing, but this would hardly be the first time that the CIA had been involved in "regime change" around the world, including in Latin and South America. Indeed, there are troubling indications that the CIA continues to be used to destabilize democratically elected governments from that of Salvador Allende in Chile to that of Hugo Chavez in Venezuela. The hypocrisy of the US government is profound.

Writing on October 28, 2002, only three days after the crash, Niman concedes that, based upon the sketchy reports he had available to him then, there was no direct evidence of foul play. But there can be no doubt of his conviction that the political motivation of the Bush administration to remove Wellstone from office had been running at a fever pitch. He concludes with somber words reflecting his—and many others'—state of mind:

> What we do know, however, is that Wellstone emerged as the most visible obstacle standing in the way of a draconian political agenda by an unelected government. And now he is conveniently gone. For our government to maintain its credibility at this time, we need to open an accountable investigation involving international participation into the death of Paul Wellstone.

International observers and investigators may have been a brilliant and innovative idea on Niman's part, but that was not to be. The NTSB investigation would fall short of the inquiry that Niman proposed, not just in its general conception but also in its execution, as we are going to ascertain.

A survey conducted by the *St. Paul Pioneer Press* the evening of the tragedy asked its readers what they believed had brought about Wellstone's death. A variety of choices, including bad weather, Al Qaeda, or an act of God were presented as choices. 69 percent of those polled chose the option, "GOP Conspiracy".

Although votes are frequently employed to arrive at decisions, the truth is not determined by polls. Indeed, the informal fallacy known as "popular sentiments" occurs when an opinion is supposed to be true because it is widely shared. On October 30th, 2002, Cherly Seal published a piece on Unknownnews.com about how she knew "in her bones, in her heart and in her soul that [Wellstone] had been murdered." What we "feel in our hearts" can serve a source of conjectures and hypotheses, but it's a blunder to suppose that feelings can substitute for reason in matters of this kind. Nevertheless, Seal was onto something when she later suggested that Wellstone's death was a refinement of the method used to take out Carnahan two years earlier. Reducing the interval of time between the hit and the election (from three weeks down to ten days) allowed less time for the Democrats to respond to the tragedy and, even more important, to make sure his wife was not available as a substitute.

The plot thickened when, on November 1, 2002, Michael Ruppert reported on his web site that he had been contacted by a specialist in the field who claimed to have inside information regarding the Wellstone case and whose words were rather chilling:

> *The day after the crash I received a message from a former CIA operative who has proven extremely reliable in the past and who is personally familiar with these kinds of assassinations. The message read, "As I have said earlier, having played ball (and still playing, in some respects) with this current crop of reinvigorated old white men, these clowns are nobody to screw around with. There will be a few more strategic accidents. You can be certain of that." (from "History Suggests It, Crash Inconsistencies Suggest It, Many, Including Some Members of Congress, Believe It", fromthewilderness.com, November 1, 2002)*

Ruppert's source, was on the inside, but there may be corroborating evidence from the outside as well. Davie Sue Cantrell lives just a few hundred yards from Camp Perry, the CIA Training Camp in Williamsburg, VA. The night before Wellstone's death, at around about 1:15 AM, she reports, (in a letter to our publisher) that she "heard a large plane take off from the runway at Camp Perry. In the previous three years of living here, I have never heard a plane take off in the middle of the night." "While this mysterious flight may have been coincidental, there is the disturbing possibility that it might have been related.

The above-cited Mike Ruppert is a former Los Angeles detective from a family with deep connections to the DIA and CIA. He also interviewed two Democratic Congressional representatives, who said they also believed that Wellstone had been murdered. One told Ruppert, "I don't think there's anyone on the Hill who doesn't suspect it. It's too convenient, too coincidental, too damned obvious."

As university professors who have undertaken investigations into this case, individually and collaboratively, both of the authors of this book understand the necessity for careful consideration of alternative hypotheses and thorough consideration of the available evidence. Indeed, among the most fundamental conditions of objectivity that govern scientific inquiries is that they must be based upon all the available relevant evidence. Evidence is relevant when its presence or absence (or truth or falsity) make a difference to the hypotheses under consideration. In this case, evidence is relevant when its presence or absence makes a difference to the truth or falsity of the hypotheses, accident or assassination, especially by making them more or less likely, given that evidence. Violating this condition, which is known as the requirement of total evidence, leads to the commission of another fallacy, "special pleading," where evidence is intentionally selected to create a biased result.

The rules of thumb that are familiar to every student of murder in the country include motive, means, and opportunity. The principal alternatives we are going to explore are (h1) *that the death was the result of an accident* and (h2) *that the death was brought about deliberately.* Distinctions must be drawn between assassinations as murders motivated for political reasons and conspiracies, which are simply crimes that are committed by two or more persons.

Conspiracies are as American as apple pie. When two guys knock off a 7/11 store, they are committing a conspiracy. Most conspiracies in this country are economic or financial, such as those involving Enron, WorldCom, and now, in relation to Iraq, Halliburton. Insider trading is an obvious, if elementary case, where Martha Stewart and her broker engaged in a conspiracy.

The standard of establishing a conclusion "beyond a reasonable doubt" has raised questions of its own, where that phrase has been taken to mean the same thing as the phrase "beyond a moral certainty." Neither, alas, sheds much light on the subject, where we shall presume that a conclusion has been established beyond a reasonable doubt when no alternative explanation is reasonable. This implies that, in the present context, we shall have established that the death of Paul Wellstone was an assassination or an accident only if we have established that no alternative explanation is reasonable. If we can prove the assassination hypothesis is reasonable but the accident hypothesis is not, then we shall have proven that his death was caused by an assassination. Otherwise, we have not.

Even proof that his death was brought about by an assassination, however, is not enough to establish that it was caused by a conspiracy, which requires additional evidence and argument. During the course of this investigation, we shall have occasion to elaborate upon the principles of scientific reasoning and to illustrate their use in other cases. We believe that Paul Wellstone, who was committed to truth as well as to justice for every human being, would approve of our inquiry, precisely because the issues are profound. They affect each and every one of us who believes in democracy and the American way or wishes they still could. We do not simply believe that Paul Wellstone was murdered by those who would benefit from his death and that those who benefit from his death are among the most powerful leaders in the political and corporate world. We believe that we have shown beyond a reasonable doubt that his death was an American assassination.

CHAPTER ONE

SOMETHING'S FISHY

> In politics nothing happens by chance. If something happens, then you
> can bet that it was planned that way.
>
> —Franklin Delano Roosevelt

At approximately 10:22 AM, on October 25, 2002, near Eveleth,
Minnesota, United States Senator Paul Wellstone, his wife, daughter,
and three staff members, as well as their pilot and co-pilot, died in
the crash of a Beechcraft King Air A-100 twin-engine airplane. The
mass media immediately blamed the weather for the crash, which
would have been appropriate had the weather been especially
difficult. During the next several days, mainstream reports of
"terrible weather" saturated the air waves. Some of the earliest reports
were emphatic, describing freezing rain, snow, and fog:

Associated Press:

   "The plane went down in freezing rain and snow."

CNN:

   *"The plane went down in snowy, frozen rain and then burst into flames.
   The weather in the Eveleth area was so bad hours after the crash that a 12
   person NTSB team was to fly from Washington into Duluth instead of
   Eveleth."*

St. Paul Pioneer Press:

> *"U.S. Sen. Paul Wellstone, the fiery, fist-shaking liberal fighting for a third term, was killed Friday morning along with his wife and daughter and five others when his twin-engine campaign plane, groping through snow and fog, crashed into a bog while landing in northeastern Minnesota."*

Three to five days later, reports of bad weather were still circulating:

Capitol Roundup:

> *"Officials said bad weather was reported in the area."*

What wasn't reported is that other planes had landed at the Eveleth-Virginia Airport that morning. When airport manager Gary Ulman heard the crash warning alarm, he had immediately taken off looking for the Senator's aircraft, in a plane of his own.

Early reports also happened to mention the swift arrival of the FBI recovery team:

ABC News:

> *"The cause of the crash was not immediately known, but sources told ABC NEWS that during the preflight weather briefing, the pilots were told they would have adverse icing conditions throughout the flight. Federal aviation officials and the FBI's evidence recovery team were at the accident scene today, probing the cause of the crash."*

Fox News:

> *"Freezing drizzle and light snow had been falling and there was light fog, but officials are not certain the weather contributed to the crash. . . The NTSB sent a nine-member team to determine the cause of the accident. At the site, FBI spokesman Paul McCabe said there was no indication the crash was related to terrorism."*

The FAA reported that:

> *"Temperature at the airport [was] 36 degrees with light snow falling at the time of the crash. Visibility was reported to be poor and icing conditions were present."*

These reports, published within two or three days of the crash, were interesting on several counts, including that an FBI spokesman announced there was no relation to terrorism, a report to which we will return shortly. Observe that a temperature of 36° Fahrenheit is well above freezing, though that ground temperature would be consistent with much lower temperatures at higher altitudes.

Initially, there was considerable optimism that light might be shed on the cause of the crash by locating the cockpit voice recorder. The *St. Paul Pioneer Press* report cited above, for example, quoted Carol Carmody, acting head of the NTSB's investigation, who had great interest in locating the recorder:

St. Paul Pioneer Press:

> "A team of 16 NTSB investigators arrived at about 8:00 PM said the board's acting chairwoman, Carol Carmody. Federal investigators were searching the crash site late Friday for the aircraft's cockpit voice recorder, Carmody said. 'There was one on the aircraft, we understand, and we're looking for that and hope that can be recovered soon.'"

CBS NEWS:

> "A 16 member team from the NTSB arrived Friday night and acting chairwoman Carol Carmody said the first priority was finding the cockpit voice recorder. The National Weather Service had issued an advisory to pilots that morning that icing was possible."

No cockpit voice recorder would be found. The search was in vain. Why would the NTSB team search for a cockpit voice recorder unless there were one? It raises the possibility that the early arrival of the FBI might have been to clean up the scene of incriminating evidence, especially the recorder.

According to Federal Regulations 14CFR135.151, planes of this general configuration are required to carry voice cockpit recorders—but only if they are required to have two pilots. This plane had two pilots, but King Air A-100s are not required to have two pilots. Hence, they are not required to have recorders.

Nevertheless, as late as Sunday, 29 October 2002, even the BBC would present a report that underscored "Freezing Rain" as a sub-heading for its story of the tragedy. In sum, the media coverage the crash received revealed at least four features that struck us as "fishy:"

- The mainstream news reports asserted early on that the crash was caused by bad weather.

- An FBI evidence recovery team was at the scene early, investigating the accident for eight hours before the NTSB team arrived.

- An FBI spokesman announced within hours that there was no evidence that the crash had been an act of terrorism.

- There were multiple conflicting reports about the NTSB team itself, which was said to have either nine, twelve, thirteen or sixteen members.

Not the least peculiar aspect of these reports is that it is contrary to NTSB policy for any other agency to assume control of crash scenes. This is something that most Americans would not know. Indeed, the FBI would issue its "conclusion" even though its spokesman would concurrently maintain that the FBI was not there to investigate the crash. Let's consider each of these issues in sequence, starting with the weather. There are reasons why diligent readers should have been skeptical of news reports.

"BAD WEATHER" AS CAUSE OF THE CRASH

Within two or three days of the crash, most ordinary folks, who tend to rely on the mainstream media, assumed the tragedy was an accident caused by bad weather. But in a *"From the Wilderness"* online newsletter article of November 2, 2002, Michael Ruppert wrote,

> *A check of more than fifty of the world's leading news organizations three days after the Wellstone crash left one clear impression: the crash had been caused by "freezing rain and snow", "limited visibility", and "likely icing of the wings."*

The apparent urge of the corporate-owned media to minimize the least controversial speculations about the crash is exemplified in CNN's Wolf Blitzer's report on the crash. According to Steve Rendall of Fairness and Accuracy in Reporting, Blitzer's reporting has a "significant tilt toward Republicans and a disproportionate number of guests who

Most of the public remember the weather being the official reason for the crash. The photo above was taken a couple miles from the crash scene 26 minutes prior to the crash.

were conservatives." It seems as if he even tried to put words into a local reporter's mouth:

> *Local reporter: There is no evidence that weather had anything to do with the crash.*
>
> *Blitzer: But the plane was flying into some sort of ice storm, was it not?*
>
> *Reporter: There is no evidence that the weather had anything to do with the crash.*

CNN quickly cut away from the report. The above conversation was deleted in the transcript's published form. In another video clip, Blitzer returns to the theme of bad weather:

> *Blitzer: We often turn to CNN's Miles O'Brien during stories like these. He's a pilot. He's very familiar with the kind of plane Senator Wellstone was on. Miles is joining us now live from Atlanta with more on that— Miles.*
>
> *Miles O'Brien, CNN Correspondent: Wolf, we got to start off as we always do with a caveat that this is obviously very early in this investigation and it would be speculative to get too far into the causes. But we can tell you what was going on in the atmosphere, and it was not a pretty day for*

flying there...Let me just explain to you why icing is a big problem. As an airplane flies through the clouds with the temperature just so, and freezing rain would be just so, the ice can build up particularly along the leading edges, on the propellers, inside the intakes for the engines, and what that can do is it reduces the aerodynamic lift of the wings, reduces the performance of the engines, can in fact take out an engine, and can put an airplane in a very difficult position, a position that is difficult to recover from...I should tell you, Wolf, that the National Transportation Safety Board's team of a dozen is on its way to the area right now in two separate aircraft. They thought they would go to Eveleth, but they chose not to. The pilots feel the weather is not good enough. They will instead fly to Duluth where there is a more precise instrument approach. So, that in and of itself is kind of telling of what's going on there right now—Wolf.

Blitzer: Telling indeed, Miles O'Brien thanks very much.

After a commercial break, Blitzer interviewed Kathleen Koch about the D.C. sniper investigation and suspects John Lee Malvo and John Allen Muhammad. End of story.

Descriptions of why icing can be a problem in general, of course, do not address whether icing was a problem on the morning of October 25, 2002, which he does not claim to know. And there were multiple possible reasons to land in Duluth rather than in Eveleth, especially when the cause of the crash had yet to be determined. Eveleth has no control tower but is equipped with a VOR/DME landing guidance system (that is, Very High Frequency Omnidirectional Range/Distance Measuring Equipment). If something were wrong with that system, it could have contributed to the crash, so it would be prudent to keep the runway closed until the system could be checked. The control tower in Duluth, about 60 miles south, monitors radar that covers Eveleth-Virginia's airspace. Another FAA radar station is located 40 miles west of Eveleth-Virginia at Nashwauk. Automated instruments at the airport at 10:14 AM CT indicated that the wind was calm and visibility was three miles in light snow. There were scattered clouds at 400 feet and overcast at 700. These reports were corroborated by a pilot on the ground who took photographs.

Even prior to the fatal crash, there were significant reasons to doubt that bad weather was probably at fault. *USA Today* talked to a pilot, Don Sipola, who said "visibility in the area at the time of the crash was 2.50 miles, well above the one-mile minimum for a standard instrument landing." Sipola also said that the crash site was south of the normal approach path so the plane must have deviated "for unknown and unexplained reasons." The wreckage was found 2.1 miles southeast of the east end of the Eveleth-Virginia Airport's Runway 27, which is itself 3 miles southeast of Eveleth, MN. The plane went down in a rather remote, swampy area.

Gary Ulman, co-owner of Taconit Aviation, based out of the Eveleth airport, took his plane up after receiving word from the Duluth tower that the Wellstone plane failed to land. "Approach called up here to me on the telephone and asked if the airplane was on the ground. And I told them 'No, it wasn't.'" said Ulman. When he went outside to double check the tarmac, he phoned the Duluth tower back to confirm that the Wellstone plane had not landed. The controller called rescue personnel, said Ulman, and he took his plane up to search for the missing flight. Ulman and other local pilots who flew into Eveleth's airport that day said icing was not at a dangerous level and characterized the weather as not dangerous.

"I don't think icing had an effect," said Ulman, who took his plane up twice after the crash, first to find the wreckage, then with Chief Shykes of the Evelyth-Virginia Fire Department to help direct the fire and rescue personnel. If there had been weather problems, Ulman would have noticed.

Nonetheless, two days after the crash, Robert Benzon, the NTSB public affairs official in charge of reporting on the investigation at this point in time, describes temperatures as "near freezing with icy and snowy conditions" at the time of the crash and was searching for "valves and cockpit switches that could indicate whether the plane's de-icing equipment was functioning." This and other inferences as to cause, however, violate the NTSB's policies. According to the NTSB web site's investigation process description, "A public affairs officer...maintains contact with the media. Confirmed, factual information is released. There is no speculation over cause."

The problem with all this reporting about bad weather being the cause of the "accident" is that reason and evidence indicate that weather was *never* a probable cause of the plane crash. A few reporters said as much, but their words were overshadowed. For example, Bill

Gardner, Phil Pina and Jim Ragsdale reported in the *St. Paul Pioneer Press* that "there was no distress call or any indication of trouble before the plane went down at about 10:20." An article in *The New York Times* on October 28, 2002 also stated that, as of the pilot's last transmission—at 10:18 AM—"there was no evidence...from the pilot's voice that there was any difficulty, no reported problems, no expressed concern." Even the FAA spokeswoman on the case said no signs of distress came from the plane's crew on its final approach.

As for the icing of the wing problem described by CNN's expert, the King Air A-100 is equipped with very effective de-icing systems. Wings and tail surfaces are equipped with pneumatic de-icing boots that inflate and deflate repeatedly to break ice from the leading edges of these surfaces. The plane's engine intakes are also protected by electric heating elements as are the propeller surfaces. The fuel is heated as well. If these systems had failed and the warning systems failed to assist the pilots in being aware of the failures, then why did they fail and why would "the weather" have been the only probable cause? Would not such failures at least have raised the question of sabotage? That question may have been finessed by the FBI.

Another fact that challenges the "bad weather" scenario is that other planes flying in the area, including another twin engine that landed earlier and reported visibility of five miles, all reported that the icing issue was not serious. In an article posted by KSTP TV, Associated Press Writer Ashley H. Grant described the Friday morning of the crash:

> On Friday, Wellstone's plane to Virginia was due to leave at 9:20 am, so he woke early and worked out at home. A former collegiate wrestler, he had a passion for fitness and insisted on exercising at least an hour most days despite a mild form of multiple sclerosis. Campaign manager Jeff Blodgett got into the office about 7:45 as usual. He took a call from the scheduler, saying the pilot was slightly concerned about the weather up north. At the same time, Gary Ulman, co-owner of Taconit Aviation, arrived at the Eveleth Virginia airport. "It was cold and a bit icy, but nothing unusual for northern Minnesota in late October. Everything was all normal, all standard," Ulman said.

National Center for Atmospheric Research meteorologist Ben

Bernstein, who studied radar and satellite imagery along with other weather information for the NTSB, told Minnesota Public Radio that icing was not likely a major problem at the time the plane crashed. "Without actually going in there with an aircraft and putting instruments and probes in there, there's no way for us to know for certain how severe the conditions may have been, but looking at the data we did look at, it didn't appear to be a particularly severe situation. This case looked like something that wasn't really far out of the norm."

The story of one of the pilots, Richard Conry, gives additional evidence of the absence of a serious weather problem. (Although other concerns were raised about this pilot, we will address them in later chapters.) According to an article by Charles Laszewski, which appeared in the *St. Paul Pioneer Press* on October 25, 2003, Conry did not like to fly in bad weather. One younger co-pilot who had flown with him even told the federal investigators after the crash that Conry had always displayed concern about icing. "Indeed, his cautious approach with regard to weather was apparently one of the reasons he had become a favorite pilot for Wellstone, who was known as a nervous flyer, especially concerned about turbulence, according to NTSB documents.... Conry always gave Wellstone a thorough weather briefing before each flight."

Evidently Conry had even considered canceling the flight when he first contacted the FAA's station in Princeton and asked for a weather report. He was told he might encounter moderating icing. But an hour afterwards, he called the FAA again and this time he was told that the situation had improved, that the wind at Eveleth was calm, visibility was three miles, light snow was falling and the cloud ceiling was at 900 feet. Conry concluded that the conditions were acceptable and filed a flight plan. "OK, that's what I need," Conry said, according to the FAA's own transcript. "At least it's above my minimum here." So the pilot was concerned to avoid even moderate icing. The weather was not the problem, as even the NTSB itself would eventually conclude.

THE FBI ON THE SCENE

The second item in the news around the world on the 25th and 26th of October was mention of an FBI rapid-response team on the scene.

Reports should also have dealt with this anomaly with a critical eye. The FBI claimed right away once on the scene that there was no sabotage. But how could the FBI possibly know that? The FBI's prompt arrival was peculiar.

Why were FBI investigators there before the NTSB? Why they were allowed to investigate the scene at all? At 9:00 AM on January 28, 2004, one of our co-authors, Four Arrows, spoke to Lauren Peduzzi, the media contact for the National Transportation Safety Board in Washington, D.C. Four Arrows asked the following questions:

> *FA: When you have a major accident, how much time elapses before you can get a team there usually?*

> *LP: For an aviation accident, we send out our team from Washington, D.C., but if it is going to take all day to get there from here we will send out someone from one of our ten regional offices.*

> *FA: Understanding that the fire and police might need to handle things until you get there, are the police allowed or encouraged to do any investigation before a team member arrives?*

> *LP: Who are you working for? Are you writing about a specific case?*

> *FA: Like I said, I'm free lancing and I want to know your policy in general.*

> *LP: Well, for aviation incidents no one is allowed to begin investigation of the scene without an NTSB member present.*

The uneasy Ms. Peduzzi was correctly quoting NTSB official policy. For fatalities in aircraft accidents, the NTSB has sole responsibility for investigations. Until they arrive, other agencies can only protect the scene and perform what is necessary to save lives. A quote from the NTSB official web site makes clear that only the NTSB can investigate air crashes:

> *In cases of suspected criminal activity, other agencies may participate in the investigation. The Safety Board does not investigate criminal activity; in the past, once it has been established that a transportation tragedy is, in fact, a criminal act, the FBI becomes the lead federal*

investigative body, with the NTSB providing any requested support...As the result of recent legislation, the NTSB will surrender lead status on a transportation accident only if the Attorney General, in consultation with the Chairman of the Safety Board, notifies the Board that circumstances reasonably indicate that the accident may have been caused by an intentional criminal act. (http://www.ntsb.gov/abt_ntsb/invest.htm)

Once it has been established that a transportation tragedy is, in fact, a criminal act, then the FBI becomes the lead federal investigative body—but only if the Attorney General notifies the NTSB that "circumstances reasonably indicate that the accident [sic] may have been caused by an intentional criminal act." So the Attorney General has a veto over whether a specific case is going to be treated as a criminal act or not.

So not only were they not supposed to be there, but the speed with which the FBI arrived is also highly suspect. According to Rick Wahlberg, Sheriff of St. Louis County, a team of FBI agents appeared at the crash site about noon. He said getting to the site was difficult, "a real unpleasant piece of property", that required all terrain vehicles. "The first responders did not make it to the scene until after 11:00." Recall that Gary Ulman said he took the fire chief up about 11:15 to find the best route to the wreck for directing other response teams. An "aircraft in possible distress" alert went out on the Eveleth local police scanner at 10:50. And at 12:10 the first formal confirmation of the crash came in from the FAA. But the FBI was already on the crash scene there.

This means the FBI recovery team was at the crash site about an hour after Gary Ulman had located the site of the wreck at 11 AM and only forty-five minutes after he had taken the fire chief up to find the best route to the wreck. This is all the more remarkable, since Eveleth-Virginia Municipal Airport is 175 miles from Minneapolis. The local residents say this is easily a two and a half hour drive, not counting the trudge through the swamp to the crash scene. Remember, just getting through the marsh to the site required ATVs, and must have been a chore all by itself. Yet the FBI was on the spot.

According to Christopher Bollyn, an investigative journalist working for the *American Free Press*, Paul McCabe, special agent and spokesman for the FBI's Minneapolis division, told him that the

FBI's Evidence Response Team (ERT) had driven to the site from the Twin Cities and arrived at the crash scene about 3:00 PM, contradicting the St. Louis County Sheriff. So when did the FBI arrive? At around 12:00 as the Sheriff reported, or at around 3:00, as the FBI spokesman claimed? Or was it "about two hours after the accident", which would have been approximately 12:30, as reported by the NTSB lead investigator, Frank Hilldrup, who referred to a statement of the "first FBI agent on the scene"? All of these conflicting reports could be false, of course, but at most one of them can be true. (See Christopher Bollyn, www.rumormillnews.net/cgi-bin/config/pl?read=25121.)

Gary Ulman confirmed the Sheriff's report to both Bollyn and Jim Fetzer that the FBI had been on the scene absolutely no later than 1:00. The Sheriff himself arrived at the site around 1:30 and saw FBI agents from the ERT whom he knew personally. When Bollyn asked Ulman if he had notified the FBI about the accident, Ulman said he had not spoken with the Bureau at any time. Asked how the FBI got to the site so quickly, Ulman said that he assumed they had come from Duluth. Bollyn's office even contacted the Duluth office of the FBI and was told that the team of recovery agents had not come from Duluth but had traveled up from the FBI office in the Twin Cities.

Both of these contradict the NTSB's Frank Hilldrup. He told Four Arrows that he talked to the first FBI agent on the scene, who told him that she arrived about two hours after the accident. He told Four Arrows she said that she was en route to another meeting in Hibbing and was told to divert to the crash site. As Ruppert and Joe Taglieri report in "Wellstone Updates: FAA, FBI, Local Officials Evasive on Key Details" (64.239.12.64/free/ww3/1127602_wellstone_update.html):

> McCabe also suggested that agents from Duluth or from Bemiji could rather easily have responded to the scene around noon but that he wasn't sure of agents' exact arrival times. When asked if logs were kept with those arrival times, McCabe said, "We don't really keep log time per se, like that, like when I write reports on whatever investigation I do, you don't put times in there. It's a day, it shows the investigation was conducted on such and such a day." Which left the matter wholly up in the air.

Lt. Tim Harkenen of the St. Louis County Sheriff's Department was the law enforcement incident commander at the scene. On November 25th, Harkenen told Ruppert and Bollyn that he would retrieve his files and look up the logged arrival times of various personnel who were at the crash site, but since that initial contact he has not taken or returned any calls. One would think that official logs would clear up the contradictions. However, Jim Fetzer reviewed the log books maintained by the Sheriff's Department at Eveleth and found them to be grossly incomplete and was unable to confirm when the FBI showed up. In response to a Freedom of Information Act request, moreover, the FAA told him that its records of private aircraft arriving in Duluth that morning were destroyed, even though they could have verified the FBI's early arrival.

More recently, efforts were made to see if the FBI actually violated NTSB policy by investigating the accident prior to the NTSB arrival. One call bore fruit. Four Arrows spoke with an Eveleth Fire Department Emergency Medical Technician, Nick Johnson. Nick was among the first rescuers to find the plane in the swampy woods. He confirmed that an Agent Decker probably arrived within two hours of the accident as Frank Hilldrup stated (although he had not given her name). Then he said that a team from Washington, D.C. arrived around 4:00 in the afternoon, and went out to the scene well before the NTSB members arrived. He read from a card one of the agents gave him. It read, "John G. Whittle. Special Agent for U.S. Capitol Police Dignitary Protection Division." This team, contrary to Hilldrups' emphatic assertion, was engaged in its own investigation at the crash scene hours before the arrival of any member of the NTSB.

Calls were made to John Malovrh, the St. Louis Country Supervising Deputy, to see if he had the exact times that the FBI showed up. People at that office would say nothing about the records and log books for that day unless it first went through him. We are still waiting for the call back. FBI spokesperson McCabe even told news reporters that the FBI was treating the site as a "crime scene" but that there were "no indications of any criminal activity" causing the crash. According to information published by Christopher Bollyn at his website, an "Evidence Response Team" worked at the scene for a significant time prior to NTSB investigators arriving from Washington that night, which occurred around 8:30 PM. The FBI ERT was from the Twin Cities. Reports conflict on the exact time of their arrival, but in any case it was well before the NTSB. This and what seemed to be efforts to deny this fact or at least the arrival time of this team are especially interesting considering that this was the same agency accused of mishandling information developed in Minneapolis that concerned 9/11 suspect Zacharias Moussaoui. This is a point to which we shall return.

Finally, it is of interest to note that according to the final NTSB report, which may be found on-line at www.ntsb.gov/publictn/2003/AAR0303.pdf, there is not even a mention that the FBI was involved in the investigation. The following is a direct quote from the appendix of this document, which runs 76 pages in it on-line form:

> Investigation
>
> The National Transportation Safety Board learned about the accident about 1130 on October 25, 2002. A go-team was assembled, and it departed that same day and arrived on scene about 2045 that evening. Accompanying the team was Acting Chairman Carol J. Carmody and representatives from the Safety Board's Offices of Government, Public, and Family Affairs.
>
> Parties to the investigation were the Federal Aviation Administration; Aviation Charter, Inc.; Raytheon Aircraft Company; and Hartzell Propeller, Inc. An accredited representative from the Transportation Safety Board of Canada and a technical advisor from Pratt & Whitney Canada also assisted in the investigation.
>
> Hearing
>
> No public hearing was held for this accident.

Four Arrows found this omission so extraordinary that, on February 19, 2004, he called Frank Hilldrup and asked him about it. Bear in mind that Hilldrup is the lead investigator for the NTSB. A transcript of their conversation now follows, namely:

> *FA: Why was the FBI not listed as party to the investigation in the final NTSB report on the Wellstone case?*
>
> *FH: They were not a party to the investigation.*

AMERICAN ASSASSINATION

FA: Then what were they doing on the scene for about 8 hours prior to the arrival of the NTSB team?

FH: I can't say for sure, since I only took over on Monday; but maybe they were there responding to the—you know—the conspiracy theories.

FA: How could there have been any conspiracy theories operating before the plane crashed?

FH: Um, well we do use police agencies to keep people away from the site… and as I said they identify bodies. Look, I have a friend who was an FBI agent on this. I'll talk to her and call you back.

FA: I'd really appreciate it. Don't you think it strange?

FH: Well, I just know everything is above board but I do want to find out.

FA: One more question. Why no public hearing for this incident?

FH: We only have hearings for high profile cases.

The lead investigator for the NTSB did not explain how he knew that "everything is above board."

The NTSB has the policy that, "Public hearings generally are held with regard to a major accident in which there is wide and sustained public interest." The crash of the most outspoken Senator in the United States Senate clearly qualifies. Hilldrup didn't explain how it possibly could not. He has not called back.

THE FBI'S OFFICIAL CONCLUSIONS

Even if reporters did not pick up on inconsistencies relating to why the FBI was on the scene for eight hours before the NTSB investigation team arrived or about how some of them got there so rapidly, someone might have asked how on earth they could have been so sure there was no foul play or terrorism involved, an assertion published in most of the newspapers around the country, such as *USA Today*, which at 7:36 PM on Friday, October 25th, 2002—the very day of the crash—published this:

> *At the site, FBI spokesman Paul McCabe said there was no indication the crash was related to terrorism. He also said it would take time to recover the bodies, which remained in the wreckage late Friday.*

Note that it was posted by *USA Today* on the web at 7:36. This means the reporter was talking to McCabe well before the NTSB had even arrived, probably closer to 6 or 6:30 at the latest, giving time for a quick report to be written. CBS would post the same quote on its site at 18:35:20. This is 6:35, meaning the reporters must have taken the report even earlier, again giving time to write and to publish the entire story.

Interestingly, McCabe's complete quote was, "Currently what I can tell you is there is no indication, nor is there is any intelligence information that would suggest that the crash of Senator Wellstone's plane was in any way related to an act of terrorism." This was spoken while the plane was still smoldering. How could he possibly know? Why, in light of a national obsession with terrorism since 9/11, would he dismiss the very possibility? Why was he there in the first place? Moreover, with all the news reports that day reminding everyone that Wellstone was "Republican enemy #1", by referring to Wellstone's "fist-shaking" opposition to every powerful money-making scheme on the Bush agenda, could not someone infer the possibility that one of the benefactors of Wellstone's death might have been responsible, even if it was not in collusion with the U.S. government? That it could have been a political assassination committed by any number of enemies?

This was such an obvious probability that it needed to be crushed quickly by the FBI. This was the sort of answer a fox might give to explain the death of the chickens. Jim Fetzer has said that he was struck by the similarity with the death of JFK where a lone person, Lee Harvey Oswald, was picked up about an hour after the assassination and charged with the crime before any investigation had been conducted. The crime occurred at 12:30 PM; a police officer named J. D. Tippit is shot around 1:10; and Oswald is arrested at the Texas Theater around 1:50 and taken to the Dallas Police Department. The official arrest record states, "This man shot and killed President John F. Kennedy and Police Officer J. D. Tippit. He also wounded Governor John Connally." The arrest was dated and timed 1:40 on November 22, 1963. Jim always thought that was pretty fast work.

Paul Wellstone himself would likely have raised the possibility that the crash was not an accident. In an article for the *St. Paul Pioneer Press* (April 27, 2001), entitled, "Wellstone Grills FBI Agents, Insists Priest was Murdered", with a sub-title, "U.S. team stands by its report on Kenya death," its staff writer, Charles Laszewski, describes how the Senator had recently accused the FBI of being wrong about the death of Reverend John Kaiser, a priest from Minnesota, whom the FBI claimed had committed suicide: "I think he was murdered. That's my own view" said the Senator.

Kaiser was an outspoken critic of the Kenyan government and its human rights violations. The FBI report said his death was "more consistent with a suicide than a homicide and that his suicide resulted with a self-inflicted gunshot wound to the head."

The FBI said Reverend Kaiser committed suicide and Senator Wellstone doubted it. Similarly, the FBI concluded that the Senator's airplane crash had nothing to do with sabotage or terrorism. We doubt that as well. We think that his death was an assassination. We will attempt to prove it was no accident.

CAROL CARMODY AND THE NTSB

Being told that the NTSB was "on the way" in many of the earliest news broadcasts also prompts concerns about time frames and why there were so many conflicting reports about the number of people on the team. Why, when NTSB investigators are on-call 24 hours—"ready to go"—did it take so long for them to get to the crash site? Were they under orders from the FBI or the U.S. Capitol Police Dignitary Protection Division? The first report that the plane was down occurred at 11: 15 AM. The first formal confirmation that it was Wellstone's plane was at 12:10. This means the NTSB arrival at 8:15 PM was eight to nine hours later. American Eagle airlines can fly from Duluth to Chicago nonstop in an hour and a half. It is at most one and a half hour drive from there. So a team member might have made it to the scene in four hours, allowing an extra hour for arrangements, considering the urgency and the federal clearance. This would have someone on the scene at 4 PM or 5 PM depending on whether they were called at 11:15 AM or 12:10 PM. Why did that not happen?

This is only a three or four-hour difference and a variety of things might have caused such a delay. However, recall that the FBI was on the scene no later than 1 PM and possibly already at noon. Either the FBI knew about the accident before the NTSB, which would in itself be strange, or else the NTSB learned about it first but gave the FBI extra time. That may violate NTSB policies, but so is allowing any other party to begin investigation of the scene without an NTSB member present. It is well known that the FBI and the NTSB partner up on aviation accidents. There are also a number of people who feel the partnership works well for covering up whatever their employer prefers to remain secret. The FBI appears to do that well.

Addressing another NTSB/FBI airplane crash investigation, for example, in an article in "Accuracy in Media," entitled "Official TWA 800 Findings Challenged," on June 10, 2002, Reed Irvine and Cliff Kicaid wrote the following revealing words:

> *The penchant of the FBI and NTSB for classifying, hiding and altering the TWA Flight 800 evidence shows that they knew the evidence did not support their findings. Last summer the NTSB, headed by a Bush appointee, secretly sold the TWA 800 wreckage, except for the mock-up of the fuselage and one engine, to a recycler. The buyer had to promise to keep it secret to get the contract.*

This issue was also exposed in an award-winning documentary, "TWA 800: The Search for the Truth." According to the film, and other articles by Irvine, the FBI withheld accounts of 278 witnesses who claimed to see a missile strike the plane that crashed on July 17, 1996, causing the death of 230 people, from the NTSB for more than a year after the crash. The results of a study to determine the origin of an alleged surface-launched object seen before the crash were ostensibly lost by the FBI. Today, those results are officially listed as simply "unable to locate" by the FBI.

James D. Sanders, author of two books on the mysterious crash of TWA 800, is also familiar with the NTSB's Carol Carmody. He frankly calls her "a political hack, willing to accommodate those who can make hers a brighter future." He told us that since the 9/11 disaster, he counts her guilty of two other egregious cover-ups. 9/11's United Flight 93 has long been rumored to have been shot down in rural Pennsylvania. Most recently author David Ray Griffin (*The New Pearl Harbor*) reported that victims on cell phones before the crash reported a military aircraft escort outside their windows.

Sanders reports that Flight 93's "fuselage was holed at least several miles prior to it crashing. Body parts, seats, along with checks and other mail in the cargo hold, was sucked through one of the engines and dumped en mass over a lake about 3 miles from the crash scene. Witnesses at the lake observed and heard the plane fly over. They immediately observed the debris dump." But then, in stepped Carol Carmody. As part of the official story that stated that Flight 93 crashed, she made the rather surprising claim that the 9 mile an hour wind blew the debris, including body parts, to the lake. "It would have taken about 20 minutes for the debris to blow from the crash site to the lake." Sanders told us.

"She lied, just as she would lie about American Flight 587 about six weeks later." Sanders points out that only a couple of months after 9/11, Flight 587 out of JFK mysteriously lost its tail and crashed in Rockaway Beach, Queens, New York City. A plane has never before lost its tail, according to aviation experts, and Sanders believes that there's "a very high probability it went down due to a small bomb onboard. Excellent witnesses describe...587 was on fire and spewing debris into the water long before it crashed. Yet, everyone from Carmody to Powell ran for the microphones to assure the public that 587 was just an accident. Those statements began less than an hour after the plane hit Rockaway Beach. The NTSB is hopelessly corrupt, as is the FBI." Sanders, a conservative, sees the NTSB as part of a new "National Security State."

There are parallels with the FBI investigation of the death of JFK here, too. Some of the most important evidence in the JFK case simply disappeared after it had been turned over to the FBI, including a triangular chunk of bone known as "the Harper fragment" from the back of the President's head. A home movie of the assassination taken from opposite the grassy knoll by a young woman named Beverly Oliver was appropriated by FBI Agent Regis Kennedy. Oliver was promised that it would be returned within two weeks. And it is a good thing that the Harper fragment was photographed before it was turned over to the FBI. The Harper fragment alone proved that JFK suffered a massive blow-out to the back of his skull and Beverly's film might have captured some of the shooters. Thanks to the FBI, both disappeared down a black hole forever.

Dr. Vernon Grose, a former NTSB Board Member, testified in Congress that "if the NTSB was doing the job they were commissioned to do by the Congress in 1967, there'd be no need for this meeting today." He outlined a brief history of the NTSB and how it was intended to be an independent body but that in 1996 it had become a political tool. He referred to documents withheld in a variety of crashes, including Value Jet 592, TWA Flight 800, American Flight 587, and the Oklahoma bombing. (Over 3,000 pages of documents appear to have been withheld by the FBI in the government's prosecution of Timothy McVeigh alone.) In all three crashes, either the NTSB or the FBI stated at the outset of the investigation—with essentially no evidence—that there had been no foul play. *Does that sound familiar? Do we have anything to learn from its history? Do these agencies exist to reveal or to conceal?*

In light of the overwhelming motivations for a political assassination of Senator Wellstone and the national concern with terrorism, it is unfortunate that so many journalists, forgetting or ignoring recent history, fail to ask important questions like those we are raising. Another is, Why did no one ask Carol Carmody, Acting Chair of the NTSB, or Robert Bezone, investigator-in-charge, why Carmody had been delegated to conduct this investigation, considering the character of her background, education, and training? American taxpayers have the right to expect that those who are responsible for conducting inquiries of the greatest importance to the nation should be well qualified.

Of special interest is Carmody's biographical sketch. First, she was chair of the hearing on the crash of American Airlines Flight 587. Taking place less than a year before the Wellstone investigation, the NTSB investigation of 587 is equally suspect. Numerous articles and dozens of eyewitnesses to the crash claim the government ignored eyewitness accounts that the Airbus 300 exploded in midair and that, not unlike the Wellstone crash, there was an unexplained fire and a broken tail section. (Tail sections do not generally break away in airline crashes that are truly accidents.) Even *The New York Times* reported, "The NTSB is not acknowledging the many eyewitness accounts of the in-flight fire or explosion, many from people who are adamant that the fire occurred before any tail or engine breakup."

AMERICAN ASSASSINATION

One would think that, unless Carmody was doing exactly what she had been ordered to do, someone else might have been sent to serve as the official government spokesperson for the Wellstone crash. And Carmody was also on the scene at the aircraft accident which killed Governor Mel Carnahan of Missouri in October 2000. Is there a pattern here?

As though this history about Carmody were not enough to warrant the image of "a fox guarding the hen house" problem, consider also that prior to joining the NTSB, she managed a firm that administered Taft-Hartley pension plans and served at the Central Intelligence Agency. Wellstone, like Idaho Senator Frank Church before him, was never afraid to question abuses of the CIA and the intelligence community. He was the most outspoken critic of the "Patriot Act," which legally obliterates the Church Committee's regulatory muzzles from the maw of U.S. intelligence, regarding the harassment and monitoring of dissent. Senator Wellstone was equally skeptical of the intelligence surrounding the 9/11 attacks and the Iraqi war resolution. To have a former CIA operative in charge of the Wellstone crash is certainly either high irony or deliberately planned.

As for the Taft-Hartly connection, it is worth noting that Taft-Hartly is considered the "slave labor act" in pro-labor camps including pro-union politicians like Paul Wellstone. Regardless of Carmody's history, readers of the many newspapers in which she gave her initial statement should have noticed her first mistake. Across the country, the news reported, as did *The Star Tribune,* that "Carmody says that her main priority would be searching for the cockpit voice recorder" as they sought to determine what happened. She said the recorder was said to be "key to learning more about the crash." The plane did not have to have one.

An FAA spokesman, Paul Takemot, said that the plane was supposed to have a cockpit voice recorder and a flight data recorder as well. According to the Federal Regulations, planes of this general configuration are required to carry voice cockpit recorders only if they are required to have two pilots. As we have explained, this plane had two pilots, but King Air A-100s are not required to have two pilots. For that reason, they are not required to have voice cockpit recorders. Of course, it is possible that Carmody was just confused and had not studied her notes about the aircraft during the eight hours before she arrived on the scene. Still, one would think that the Acting Chair of NTSB with more than 20 years experience with the aviation community, including eleven years at the FAA, would know about such things. Or did she know something that we don't know?

If this plane, which was leased through Charter Aviation, Inc., had carried a voice cockpit recorder, even though it was not required to do so, that would explain quite a lot about the sudden appearance of the FBI. Under circumstances of this kind, if some sort of skullduggery was afoot, it would have been indispensable to cover up the true causes of the crash by cleaning up the site as soon as possible and before any foolish civilian decided to "help out." Imagine how embarrassing it would have been to have to explain the contents of the cockpit voice recorder if the plane had been taken down. It would have been as awkward as if the existence of the Harper fragment had become a matter of public knowledge or if a film of the assassination had actually included footage of an assassin firing shots from other than the "official sniper's lair".

There is another alternative. While the plane was not required to carry a voice recorder, it might still have been equipped with one by Charter Aviation, Inc. King Airs are expensive to own and costly to maintain, but are comfortable and accommodating. They attract very high-class and well-to-do clients. Under these conditions, the FBI might have rushed to the scene in the belief that recorders were on board. Jim Fetzer took an alternative route and called one of its owners to ask him whether the plane had been equipped with recorders of either kind. The owner, who was aware of his suspicions that the crash might have been an assassination, was not happy to hear from him and vehemently denied that the plane was equipped with them. "They are expensive and they aren't required and they weren't on the plane.", he was told. But the FBI might not have known or else couldn't leave it to chance. It's difficult to reconcile its early arrival with an accident.

Carmody's second mistake might have been her announcement that she expected the medical examiner's post-mortems to be completed by Sunday, two days after the crash. This would seem reasonable, of course, but as we will find in a later chapter, this was also far off the mark. Perhaps such errors were only the result of overwork and a lack of training. In 1999, the Rand Institute for Civil Justice completed a review of NTSB's practices and procedures in major aviation accidents. This study found that NTSB investigators were being overworked and weren't receiving adequate training to keep pace with the technical complexities of aviation accidents, resulting in an over-reliance on subject-matter expertise from others. (See Cynthia Lebow, "Safety in the Skies: Personnel and Parties in NTSB Aviation Accident Investigations.")

Perhaps Carmody and the other nine, ten, twelve, thirteen or sixteen NTSB team members, whatever the correct number may have been, are completely innocent of any cover-up and, because of under-training and fatigue, they simply relied on the expertise of the FBI, the agency that, in spite of NTSB policy, investigated the crash for most of the day before the NTSB team, probably exhausted from their trip, had even arrived on the scene. That would still not explain the early arrival of the FBI, but it might tend to exonerate the NTSB, an issue to which we shall return. It will take the NTSB thirteen months to produce a report on the Wellstone crash. Before we analyze it specifically, however, let us next look at a most important question, the matter of motive. If a person or persons arranged for Senator Paul Wellstone's assassination, the motivation to do so would have had to have been very great.

CHAPTER TWO

MOTIVES FOR MURDER

Even the strongest flame cannot burn in a drenching downpour.
—Senator Paul Wellstone

In an MSN article entitled, "Did the Stock Market Rally Because Sen. Wellstone Died?" posted Friday, October 25th 2002, about eight hours after Senator Wellstone's plane crashed, Daniel Gross, who authors an on-line daily column on business and finance, wrote,

> Did the market rally Friday afternoon because Sen. Paul Wellstone, (D-MN), one of the nation's most honest and useful public servants, died in a plane crash? You won't find any analysts making this case on CNBC this afternoon, on Wall Street Week With Fortune tonight, or in Barron's tomorrow...Repulsive as it may be, I can't help but think that it did. The Dow rose steadily after the news of the crash came over the wires, eventually closing up 127 points on the day. . . .

> For proof that it was Wellstone's death and not any other news that moved the market, just pull up an intra-day chart on the Dow. You'll see that it was meandering around lazily for much of the day, down 30 in the morning, up 40 in the afternoon. At 1:30 it was basically flat...At 1:31 came the first word that Wellstone was likely on board. TV news channels jumped on the news. At 1:50, the Associated Press reported that Wellstone had died. Now look at that intra-day chart of the Dow again.

From 1:50 to the close of the day, the Dow went crazy. Gross concludes that investors who were savvy about what it would mean to corporate profits for the Senate to come under control of the Republicans were responsible. The death of a Senator implied huge corporate advantages. Indeed, Wellstone's demise, together with the suspicious loss of Senator Max Cleland in Georgia, cleared the way for Republican control of the United States Congress. According to Jeffrey McMurray in a piece for the *Associated Press,* shortly after the Minnesota tragedy,

> *Georgia defied its traditions of long-tenured senators and Democratic governors, replacing Sen. Max Cleland after just one term in a Republican landslide...Rep. Saxby Chambliss' victory Tuesday over Cleland helped the GOP recapture the Senate.*

Cleland, a venerated Democrat and war hero, was defeated for re-election in Georgia in one of the nastiest campaigns of 2002. Moreover, it is likely that Wellstone's death played a significant role. Thus, the day after the crash, the Republicans transferred $700,000 to be used against Cleland, money that they had planned to use against Wellstone in Minnesota. The reaction to the funeral, where distraught Democrats, especially Wellstone's campaign manager, became carried away in an emotional pitch to carry his message forward—an event that was subjected to massive and unfair "spin" by conservative commentators who had not seen the event—angered many Republicans and, undoubtedly, inspired anti-Democratic efforts and votes.

How far the Bush machine is willing to go to exert its control was revealed by the fiasco in Florida and, more ominously, may encompass the use of electronic voting machines, a concern that is virtually certain to be heightened during the 2004 elections. With electronic voting machines, there's no paper trail, which means no recount is possible. Although we have not seen the case argued, surely this method of counting votes could not pass Constitutional scrutiny. After all, if an election is disputed, there is no way to verify the original count. This appears to be a clear violation of the due process and equal protection provisions of the Constitution. Stalin observed that it doesn't matter who casts the votes but who counts them. When counts are cloaked in secrecy, democracy takes a heavy hit.

All three companies that make these voting machines refuse to allow security experts to analyze their software to make sure that they are secure. This is an entirely absurd situation. As anyone familiar with computer science is aware, the kinds of programs for counting votes are among the most elementary and obvious known to the discipline: simply take an existing number n and add 1 to it for each vote cast for each candidate. If there is anything proprietary about these programs, it must be the software that would allow for the redistribution of votes from some candidates to others or for the substitution of a predetermined number of votes for each candidate. The very idea that the software for voting machines should not be open for inspection and verification by representatives of the parties and the people is a stellar instance of the most blatant "in your face" theft of democracy imaginable.

Anyone taken in by the deceitful argument that the technology does not exist to create fail-safe machines for this purpose has not been paying attention to modern technological developments. ATMs, among the most secure devices known to man, are manufactured by Diebold, a firm that claims to be unable to produce safe voting machines. The largest of the three companies who make all of these machines, ES&S, is even owned by Howard Ahmanson, a very right-wing benefactor of the Christian reconstructionist movement, whose followers wish to turn certain tenets of the Bible into international law. According to *The Hill*, a respected Washington, DC publication, Chuck Hagel, former conservative radio talk-show host and now Republican Senator from Nebraska, was the past head of and continues as part owner of ES&S, which counted most of the votes in his own election.

A HUNTED MAN

Another strange death in an airplane crash helped set the stage for a Republican victory in 2002. As readers may recollect, Governor Mel Carnahan died in an earlier October plane crash, this one in Missouri three weeks prior to the election of 2000, a bitter campaign against the Republican Senator, John Ashcroft. Even after his death, however, Carnahan collected enough votes to beat Ashcroft and Carnahan's wife, Jean, was appointed to the Senate. The next month, Bush named Ashcroft, the darling of the religious right, as his choice for US Attorney General. His confirmation to that position was hung by a thread and was ultimately determined by Jim Jefford's decision that George Bush was entitled to his preference for Attorney General. But in 2002, Jean Carnahan would lose her bid for election in her own right to Republican Jim Tenet.

Throughout 2001, George Bush made terminating Wellstone's senate career his foremost priority. By October 2002, he had visited Minnesota four times to drum up support for his hand-selected candidate, former St. Paul Mayor Norm Colemen. Large sums of money were being funneled into the state to unseat Wellstone, including one million dollars for advertisements attacking Wellstone that was put up by an anonymous group calling itself "Americans for Job Security." By most accounts, the race between the candidates was very close. They were running neck-and-neck.

Wellstone then became the first and only senator running for re-election to vote against the Bush "use of force" resolution for unilateral action against Iraq. He once again voted his conscience, in spite of Vice President Cheney's blatant strong-armed tactics to gain support for the war. At a meeting with war veterans in Willmar, MN, two days before his death, Wellstone said that Cheney had told him, "If you vote against the war in Iraq, the Bush administration will do whatever is necessary to get you. There will be severe ramifications for you and the state of Minnesota." Wellstone, knowing his position could well cost him his political career, spoke eloquently on the floor of the Senate, October 11, 2002:

> The intense cooperation of other nations in matters related to intelligence sharing, security, political and economic cooperation, law enforcement and financial surveillance and other areas has been crucial to this fight and enables us to wage it effectively with our allies. Over the past year, this cooperation has been our most successful weapon against terror networks. That, not attacking Iraq, should be the main focus of our efforts in the war on terror. . . . I believe many Americans still have profound questions about the wisdom of relying too heavily on a pre-emptive go-it-alone military approach. Acting now on our own might be a sign of our power. Acting sensibly, in a measured way in concert with our allies, with bipartisan congressional support, would be a sign of our strength.

Instead of hurting his popularity, the polls indicated that his position moved him ahead of his rival. A Minneapolis *Star Tribune* poll of around a thousand likely voters surveyed the week of October 11th 2002 showed that 47 percent supported Wellstone and only 41 percent favored Coleman. This had to have been a shock to the Bush administration, threatening its image as an invincible political machine.

Of course, these statistics did not guarantee victory for Wellstone. He had been diagnosed with a mild form of multiple sclerosis and, even though doctors said it would not affect his ability to work long hours or serve a third term in the Senate, some voters might have been reluctant to give him a third term. Other folks were even upset with him for seeking a third term at all, because he had once said that was something he would not do. The stakes were very high, however, and those who stood to gain billions of dollars in defense contracts, oil profits, deregulation, and corporate-welfare-related financial benefits were worried. It was no secret that Wellstone was the Republicans'—including Wall Street's—political enemy #1. For example, a column by John Nichols in the Madison, Wisconsin, *Capital Times* on April 24, 2001 had this to say about the perception of Wellstone from the Bush White House:

> *Let there be no doubt as to the identity of George W. Bush's least favorite Democratic U.S. senator. It's Wellstone, the rabble-rousing Progressive who represents what remains of the fighting populist spirit of the Upper Midwest.*
>
> *As Wellstone prepares to seek a third term next year, it would be reasonable to assume that he might finally be in for some smooth political sailing. But reasonableness doesn't figure into the calculations of the Bush White House, where the president himself, Vice President Dick Cheney and political commissar Karl Rove practice the politics of vengeance.*
>
> *The Bushies despise Wellstone, who unlike most Senate Democrats has been fighting spirited battles against the new administration's policies on everything from the environment to the tax cuts for the rich to military aid for the "Plan Colombia" drug war boondoggle. The Bush camp has been focusing highest-level attention on "Plan Wellstone"—its project to silence progressive opposition. What does Wellstone say?*
>
> *"I think the way to oppose George W. Bush is to stand up to him, to speak out when his policies are wrong, to put holds on bad legislation he's promoting. Obviously, that's not the sort of opposition Bush and Cheney approve of. The nice thing is that, even if they can dictate the Republican nominee, the people of Minnesota still get to choose their senator."*

Similar sentiments abounded. On April 28th, 2002, for example, *USA Today* wrote:

> Tim Pawlenty, majority leader of the Minnesota House of Representatives, was about to announce a challenge of Democratic Senator Paul Wellstone last spring when Cheney asked him not to run. That left the field clear for former St. Paul mayor Norm Coleman, a candidate the White House believed had a better chance of winning. Coleman was planning to run for governor before a call from Bush persuaded him to switch races. Now Pawlenty is running for governor.

In Washington, D.C., *The Washington Post*, May 11th, 2002, published the following:

> Besides Wellstone and Coleman, no one may have a greater stake in the race than Bush and Vice President Cheney, who have taken a more prominent role than many of their predecessors in recruiting Senate candidates...and nowhere more conspicuously than in Minnesota... (Wellstone's) defeat would erase the Democrats' one-vote majority and put the Senate back under Republican control. So Wellstone, once the quintessential outsider, becomes a linchpin of the power balance in Washington.

In a column published in *The Nation* on May 9th, 2002, titled, "Paul Wellstone, Fighter," John Nichols advanced reasons why Paul Wellstone was "a hunted man". "Minnesota's senior senator is not just another Democrat on White House political czar Karl Rove's target list," Nichols wrote. "Rather, getting rid of Wellstone is a passion for Rove, Dick Cheney, George W. Bush and the special-interest lobbies that fund the most sophisticated political operation ever assembled by a presidential administration."

"If he wins, a blow will be struck, not just against the Bush machine but against those in the Democratic Party who argue for tepid moderation." The possibility that, in addition to maintaining the Democrat's plurality in the Senate, Wellstone's success might also motivate the party to follow his lead in opposing Bush, would have been an even greater motive for murder, considering the implications. When JFK was taken out, the conspirators most feared the President might survive and unleash the full powers of his office to track them down. It does not take a great leap of faith to envision a situation in which Bush's closest advisors conclude that a victorious Wellstone, like a wounded President, would be a calamity of the

AMERICAN ASSASSINATION

highest order that must be avoided no matter what the cost. If that meant an attempt to kill him, it was a risk that they would have to run.

The potential for Wellstone to upset Republican control of the Senate is only one reason for wanting to get rid of him. It ought to be remembered that Wellstone was also chairman of the new securities reform committee. And it was Wellstone who was attempting to block the nomination of William Webster, former CIA and FBI head and a "best friend" of big business and of big accounting firms, to be the new chairman of the SEC's Accounting "Oversight Commission." Another consideration relates to the presidential election of 2004. Would Wellstone have had a better chance to beat Bush than any other Democratic candidate? Jim Farrell gave his answer to this question in the very title of a piece that he contributed to *The Nation:* "Dean's No Wellstone."

Wellstone had also indicated an interest in running for the 2004 presidency. The political action committee MoveOn PAC had already collected more than half a million dollars for his Senate re-election campaign, and there were separate discussions about a run for the White House. He had the most consistent record of opposing Bush administration initiatives of any member of the Senate. He received 100% ratings from the AFL-CIO, the Americans for Democratic Action, and the League of Conservation Voters. The *Star Tribune* described him appropriately as "the go-to guy to advance the causes of educators, environmentalists, consumer and labor groups, the elderly and the poor." Wellstone could have returned the Democrats to their base: working families, passionate progressives, and activists who shared Wellstone's vigor and verve. In contrast, the Democratic rebuttals following George W. Bush's 2004 State of the Union address, failed to even mentioned Bush's pathetic environmental record.

No one talked about the financial motive for the war in Iraq. Wellstone would have addressed it. Bush policy allows "homeland security" corporate contracts to be signed with American companies that have moved offshore to avoid US taxes. Wellstone had loudly opposed this unpatriotic hypocrisy. He was outspoken about US involvement in Columbia. Displaying his knack for standing up to political pressure, he was one of a handful of senators opposing plan that (in theory) directed a $1.3 billion in funds against drug trading in Columbia. He said he would insist that Columbia get no more US aid until it improved its human rights record. Indeed, an assassination attempt on his life may have occurred while he was in Columbia, an event we discuss below.

Wellstone's outspoken position on W.R. Grace Asbestos also ruffled powerful feathers. Wellstone, along with Senators Baucus, Cantwell, Murray, and Dayton, introduced legislation to improve protections for workers and consumers against asbestos poisoning. Wellstone was a powerful opponent of W.R. Grace and Co., the owner of the Libby vermiculite mine that produced the Zonolite insulation in homes across the country, with 53,505 in Washington alone. Grace had once run a plant in Wellstone's state, where vermiculite thorium, which is a radioactive element, and contaminants in the ground had been linked to serious health problems there. On January 29, 2001, the *Business Journal* reported the situation was rather grave:

> *Asbestos-related litigation continues to plague W.R. Grace & Co. For the fourth quarter ended Dec. 30, Grace had a net loss of 107.6 million or 1.65 per share, compared to a net income of 48.2 million or 66 cents per share. For the 2000 fourth quarter, the company had sales of 384.4 million. "Asbestos litigation continues to be our company's biggest challenge," said Grace CEO and Paul J. Norris. "During 2000 we have seen the litigation environment worsen and become more uncertain."*

Vice President Cheney is deeply vested in the asbestos issues. Within three years of the sale of a company he sold without disclosing its asbestos liabilities, his insurance company, Highlands, found itself saddled with 23,000 claims worth about $80 million from workers at Halliburton's Brown & Root construction subsidiary. Cheney was also involved in a $7.7 billion merger with Dresser Industries, a merger that had almost bankrupted Halliburton because of Dresser Industries' own asbestos liabilities. Halliburton had estimated that its asbestos liability was about $2.2 billion over a 15 year period starting in 1998. Highlands filed suit in Delaware in 2000 but Highlands' lawyers were unable to depose Cheney because he had already begun his new job as vice president of the United States. Cheney-Ashcroft-Hyde could only have benefited by removing the pressure that Senator Paul Wellstone had been applying. The total litigation potential would make the Enron scandal look relatively benign.

COLLATERAL FRINGE BENEFITS

Once again, Wellstone seems to have been a nemesis for big business. However, Wellstone posed an even more significant and costly threat to corporate profit-making interests. He tried to enable the 2002 defense appropriation's bill to bar corporate tax dodgers from being eligible for defense department contracts. Additionally, he successfully amended the Homeland Security bill to bar those companies from getting contracts with the new "Department of Homeland Security." Both amendments passed on the Senate floor by voice votes.

After the November election—and after Paul Wellstone's tragic death—the final version of the homeland security bill gutted the Wellstone amendment. His bills were obliterated by enough waivers to assure that corporate lobby groups would indeed land the billion-dollar defense contracts we have now seen, especially in Iraq. Similarly, a mental health reform Wellstone had championed, which would have required insurance companies to provide mental health coverage on a par with physical health coverage if their policies cover both, has been successfully blocked, one more indication that the loss of "the conscience of the Senate" continues to make a difference.

So it appears Wellstone, as the only Democratic candidate with the courage and conviction to take on such issues, would likely have gained tremendous support for the Democratic nomination in light of increasing public awareness about the Bush administration's deceptions, which have been documented in numerous best-selling books like Greg Palast's *The Best Money Democracy Can Buy,* Michael Moore's *Stupid White Men,* and Al Franken's *Lies and the Lying Liars that Tell Them,* to name a few. Others, of course, are far more ominous and reach back in time to provide an history of the family that stretches from Prescott Bush to George Herbert Walker Bush up to George W. Bush, such as Kevin Phillip's *American Dynasty.* It is not a pretty picture.

It would also benefit the search for truth about whether Wellstone's death was an accident or an assassination to consider the character and historical actions of the Bush regime, many which Wellstone himself was questioning. Even as we compose these sentences, NPR is running a story about an investigation of Halliburton for an 180 million dollar bribe for an overseas natural gas contract that took place when (now Vice-President) Dick Cheney was at Halliburton's helm. Any study of motives for a crime of this kind should consider character and values. By looking briefly at a handful of the stories earning the "most censored story" award from Sonoma State University's "Project Censored," a 27-year old program dedicated to bringing to light previously censored news stories, we gain insight into both Bush administrations.

An article by David Armstrong, for example, revealed that a 1992 classified internal policy study entitled, "Defense Planning Guidance", called for the U.S. to assert its military superiority to prevent the emergence of a superpower rival. It called for the U.S. to diversify its military presence throughout the world and offered a policy of preemption, foreseeing the need for the U.S. to act alone. Another report described by Armstrong and released by the Project for the New American Century in 2000 suggested the U.S. needs a catastrophe, "a new Pearl Harbor," to jump start the blueprint for military and economic world dominance. PNAC was founded by Cheney, Wolfowitz, Richard Perle, Donald Rumsfeld and other cronies of Bush senior.

An article by Michael I. Niman, who, as we've already mentioned, suspected Wellstone had been taken out, exposed the fact that the Bush administration insiders illegally removed 8000 pages from a declaration the Iraqi government had submitted to the UN and the International Atomic Energy Agency about its weapons programs. The practice of this technique of "special pleading"—selecting evidence favorable to your side and eliminating the rest—appears to be typical of this administration, which wants to have its way no matter what, even if that requires lying, cheating, or killing.

Another article by Chris Floyd discussed a new entity: "According to a classified document prepared for Rumsfeld by his Defense Science Board, the new organization— The Proactive, Preemptive Operations Group—will carry out secret missions designed to stimulate reactions among terrorists groups, provoking them into committing violent acts which would then expose them to counteraction by U.S. forces." This technique is reminiscent of a question that has arisen in the course of research on the death of JFK —where most of the evidence that was used to incriminate Lee Harvey Oswald in the assassination was planted, fabricated, or manufactured—which is this: Why would it be necessary to frame a guilty man? Provoking groups into committing violent acts looks a lot like creating phony pretexts that might cause them to do things that they might not do absent the provocation. But it could be extremely valuable politically.

An article by Lee Sustar showed how the new Bush administration has used the Department of Homeland Security to make unions disappear and to dismantle pay scales, bans on discrimination, whistle-blower protections and collective bargaining rights. These aspects of "homeland security" are not reported in the national press. And an article by Dan Kapelovitz drew the connection between the so-called "Gulf War Syndrome" and the use of depleted uranium weapons—which probably are in violation of international law—and how both Bush administrations continue to use these weapons, knowing full well that they are making sick or killing thousands of U.S. service men and women, not to mention millions of innocent victims in Kosovo, Bosnia, Afghanistan and Iraq. This is an international disgrace that dishonors the nation. Every citizen of this country should be offended at the use of such weapons.

An article by Duncan Campbell and Greg Palast described how the George W. Bush administration was behind the failed military coup in Venezuela—where its efforts continue to this day. Another article by Greg Palast described the corruption that led to tens of thousands of Democratic voters being illegally removed via instructions from Jeb Bush in the infamous Florida election scandal that gave the White House to his brother George. And another article in *The Nation*, May 27, 2002 described Paul Wellstone as the lead voice in pushing for an investigation into a missing 350 million dollars from the Bureau of Indian Affairs. Bush's Secretary of Interior Gale Norton has twice taken the Fifth Amendment and refused to answer questions about where the money has gone. She remains in her position to this day, a nice example of the Bush plan for restoring "honor and dignity" to the office of President of the United States.

Such stories are but the tip of the iceberg, but they reveal the extreme violations of law, human rights, environmental protections, and human life our government has demonstrated and that Wellstone was challenging. The fact that the U.S. government has historically been responsible for murdering and assassinating people, then lying about it through its teeth, speaks as much to motive as it does to the actual barriers that Wellstone represented to special interest groups. Beginning with its genocidal policies against American Indians, up through Viet Nam and the invasion of Panama, to its hushed support for the brutal decimation of a third of the population of East Timor, its support of the brutal Pinochet, and its current deceptions relating to wars against Afghanistan and Iraq, U.S. covert operations have helped to kill millions, not to mention American service men and women. In Iraq, we don't even keep count.

The Association for Responsible Dissent estimates that by 1987, some six million people had already died as a result of CIA cover operations. William Blum, a former State Department official refers to this history as "an American Holocaust." Here are some examples from the list compiled by Steve Kangas in his "Mirrors" article, which is titled, "A Timeline of CIA Atrocities." (A more extensive list from 1776 to 2003 is available in Ward Churchill's 2004 book, *On the Justice of Roosting Chickens*.)

- 1947: President Truman sends military aid to Greece to support right-wing forces fighting communist rebels.

- 1948: CIA corrupts democratic elections in Italy when communists threaten to win elections.

- 1952: In Iran, the CIA overthrows democratically elected Mossadegh in a military coup after he threatened to nationalize British oil and replaces him with a dictator, the Shaw of Iran, whose secret police are brutal and kill many.

- 1954: In Guatemala, CIA overthrows democratically elected Jacob Arbenz in a military coup. Arbenz has threatened to nationalize the Rockefeller-owned Fruit Company in which CIA Director Allen Dulles owns stock. Arbenz is replaced with a series of right-wing dictators whose brutal policies will kill over 100,000 Guatemalans.

- 1954-58 CIA attempts to overthrow the communist government of North Vietnam.

- 1957-73 CIA carries out about one coup per year to nullify Laosian democratic elections. CIA defeats result by U.S. dropping more bombs than it did in WWII. A quarter of all Laotians become refugees.

- 1958 U.S. military helps put into place Duvalier as dictator of Haiti. His police will kill more than 100,000 and the U.S. does not protest their dismal human rights record.

- 1963 CIA overthrows democratically elected President Juan Bosch in a military coup in the Dominican Republic, and installs a repressive, right-wing junta. The same thing happens in Ecuador.

- 1964 In Brazil, a CIA-backed military coup overthrows the democratically elected government of Joao Goulart. The junta that replaces it will become among the most bloodthirsty in history.

Similar horrors continue in Indonesia, Greece, the Congo, Bolivia, Uruguay, Cambodia, Chili, Angola, Iran, Afghanistan, El Salvador, Nicaragua, Honduras, etc.

(see http://mirrors.korpios.org/resurgent/CIAtimeline.html)

GOVERNMENT BY ASSASSINATION

One of the most recent and clear indictments of the CIA is found in the National Security Archives' book by Peter Kornbluh, *The Pinochet File* (2004). Through an amazing and exceptionally lucky effort, NSA's staff managed to get, under the Clinton administration, thousands of government records about the U.S. involvement in Chile declassified. In this book, the authors reveal records of the highest ranking leaders of the U.S., including especially Henry Kissinger and Richard Nixon. These records show beyond any doubt that the U.S. directly orchestrated the overthrow of a democratically elected official and put into place and supported for years a brutal dictator, whose atrocities and human rights violations have become infamous.

It also clearly shows the efforts of the President, the Secretary of State, the CIA and the White House to conceal the truth from the

American people. If the powers that be were so afraid that a democratically-elected socialist would hurt corporate interests in Latin America that they would encourage virtual genocide and lie about it, why would one be hesitant to consider their willingness, especially considering the character of those in power today, to kill eight people to possibly prevent the rise of the most powerful enemy of the White House? This White House has compounded lie upon lie to manipulate the American people into supporting a war in Iraq that the simple truth would not have justified. In Iraq, there were no weapons of mass destruction, no ongoing terrorist activities, and no ties to 9/11. This is not tangential to the case about the strange untimely death of Senator Wellstone. An administration that would lie to send hundreds of thousands of young American men and women into harm's way is not an administration that would hesitate to kill a single senator.

More and more we are learning about such deceits as they relate to a government that is controlled by special interest groups. For example, in a recent interview, our Vice President, Dick Cheney, touted a report and leaked classified documents that the administration itself billed as "inaccurate" as evidence for claiming there was a Iraq-Al Qaeda connection. When questioned about his assertion of a partnership between Saddam Hussein and Al Qaeda, Cheney offered the following response as an answer:

> *You ought to go look at an article that Stephen Hayes did in the* Weekly Standard *here a few weeks ago, that goes through and lays out in some detail, based on an assessment that was done by the Department of Defense and forwarded to the Senate Intelligence Committee some weeks ago. That's your best source of information.*

But the article and document Cheney cited was discredited by the administration as "inaccurate" two month previously. A January 23, 2004 article in *The Los Angeles Times* also reports that intelligence has revealed that neither the Iraqis nor Al Qaeda trusted one another enough to establish a relationship. Which is hardly surprising, since Saddam represented the kind of secular government that Osama bin Laden has sworn to depose. These kinds of discrepancies and outright lies are ever so gradually becoming more and more conspicuous to Americans on both sides of the political isle.

Thus, it is not a stretch to entertain the prospect that a government with such a record as these items reveal might use whatever means are necessary to accomplish its corrupt goals, including taking out a senator and his family in exchange to extend continued wealth and power. The same might be said about corrupt leaders of large corporations in light of the many corporate scandals coming to light. How can anyone not take seriously the questions that are posed here? Despite our illusions, these are sorts of things that also happen in America, where the death of JFK is only the most stunning illustration. We know it happens elsewhere around the world. We are told it doesn't happen here, but that's merely a myth that manipulates the American people.

Those familiar with studies such as Peter Dale Scott, *Deep Politics and the Death of JFK* (1993), and Robert Schramm Burnside, *Coup D'Etat* (2003), have an idea how it was done in the case of JFK, whose assassination was no more than "an adjustment" to preserving the status quo with respect to the distribution of both wealth and power. An on-line article, "Deep Black Lies: Reporting on Crime and Corruption in High Places," by an English author and investigative journalist, David Guyatt, makes the point, which most Americans do not grasp, as follows:

> *Fraud, manipulation, grand larceny on a scale that is almost unimaginable to comprehend—and cold blooded murder when things look like they are about to unravel—are the daily bread and drink of these financial titans. If someone gets out of order or is perceived to be a threat, even if he is a member of the club, he is taken care of in the classical Roman way.*

Paul Wellstone was a threat to the status quo. He was doing all he could to make life better for the weak, the poor, and the powerless. He was tireless and energetic to a fault in criticizing those who perpetuate inequality and injustice and multiple levels of corruption and in pursuing what he perceived to be a better life for us all. The threat was real and it was "in their face". We believe he died for it. Those who profit from a crime are those most likely to have done it. There were powerful motives for taking this man out.

OTHER SUSPICIOUS DEATHS

Senator Wellstone's death counts as one among many suspicious deaths of very prominent political figures. A database about dead U.S. politicians on the Internet includes some 47 who have died in disasters or airplane crashes during the 20th Century
(http://politicalgraveyard.com/death/aircraft.html).

Michael Ruppert has shown that, of 22 air crashes involving state and federal officials, 64% were Democrats and 36% Republicans. Six fatalities occurred during election campaigns. If our thesis is correct, Wellstone was not the first political assassination by airplane.

Governor Mel Carnahan was the second Missouri politician to die in a small plane crash. The first was Democratic Representative Jerry Litton, whose plane crashed the night he won the Democratic nomination for senate in 1976. His Republican opponent ultimately captured the seat.

Sitting U.S. Senator, liberal Republican John Heinz, liberal Republican of Pennsylvania, and an outspoken critic of the Vietnam War, died in a plane crash. His death occurred during the administration of George Herbert Walker Bush, and was as odd as Wellstone's. It came about on April 4, 1991 when the landing gear on his plane malfunctioned and the helicopter dispatched to survey the problem in turn crashed into his plane. A progressive voice for health care and social services, public transportation, and the environment, his wife, Tereza, would subsequently marry another prominent liberal politician who was also an outspoken critic of the Vietnam war, this time a Democrat from Massachusetts named John Kerry.

Former Senator John Tower, chair of the commission which investigated the Iran/Contra scandal, also died in a small plane crash.

Another member of a prominent government commission who died in a small plane crash was former Democratic representative and House Majority Leader Hale Boggs. Boggs was best known as one of the seven members of the Warren Commission, which investigated the assassination of President John F. Kennedy. Boggs had "strong doubts" that the assassin acted alone, but went along with the commission findings. Later, in 1971 and 1972, he went public with his doubts. He was presumed dead after the small plane carrying him and Democratic Representative Nicholas Begich disappeared in 1972.

Texas Democratic Representative Mickey Leland also died in a plane crash. In his case, the six-term member of Congress and outspoken advocate of sanctions against the apartheid government of South Africa, died while traveling in Ethiopia. Another American politician to die overseas in a plane crash was the Clinton administration's Commerce Secretary, Ronald Brown, whose plane went down in the Balkans.

Panamanian General Omar Torrijos, who in 1981 threatened to destroy the Panama Canal in the event of a U.S. invasion. Torrijos died shortly thereafter when the instruments in his plane failed to function upon takeoff. Panamanians speculated that the U.S. was involved in the death of the popular dictator. Torrijos was replaced by the CIA asset Manuel Noriega, who previously worked with George Herbert Walker Bush.

Nebraska Private Investigator Gary Caridori was investigating the Franklin Savings & Loan debacle, top Republican Lawrence King, and a call-boys scandal involving "top levels" of the first Bush White House when his small-engine plane crashed on July 11, 1990. Caridori had been harassed for months beforehand, and the FBI seized his papers the day after his death. The "Franklin Cover-Up" remains one of the least-reported major scandal stories of the past two decades. A documentary on the topic was pulled from Discovery Channel's schedule at the last minute.

These are examples that raise the prospect that murder may have been used selectively over the past 30 years to "resolve" political problems. We do not know how many of these cases were genuine cases of assassination, but their occurrence strongly suggests that the possibilities are genuine. Each case deserves serious investigation. But it would be too much to expect the U.S. government to conduct open and honest inquiries into the death of political figures when the government itself is involved. Perhaps the most telling indication of complicity by the government thus appears to be the discovery that the truth has been obscured by a cover-up involving the government, since there would appear to be no other reason for covering-up these crimes. Employing deceit and deception to obfuscate their occurrence undermines democracy and Constitutional government and are acts of treason upon the nation.

In this respect, Senator Paul Wellstone must have been an extremely tempting target. Wellstone was defying the odds. He was pulling away from Norm Coleman, the hand-picked candidate of Karl Rove. The differences between them could hardly have been greater. His lead had grown t o between 6 and 8 points and was increasing. Cheney had warned him that the Bush administration will do whatever is necessary to get you. *There will be severe ramifications for you and the state of Minnesota.*

The situation was serious. To the White House, this guy was a menace. He might have filibustered the Homeland Security Act. He opposed them on tax cuts, the SEC, and the war on Iraq. He wanted to investigate 9/11. In the Senate, he had become an obstacle to the exercise of power. Are there any conceivable "ramifications" that could have been more severe than assassinating the Senate's most liberal member? The political motives for taking him out appear to have been simply overwhelming.

CHAPTER THREE

GATHERING EVIDENCE

> The evidence has to be unambiguous and strong.
>
> —Senator Paul Wellstone

Let's look closer at information that illuminates the Wellstone tragedy. After more than a year of analysis, the NTSB ignored the majority of this evidence in their final report. A *USA Today* article published on February 23, 2003 reported that "Steven Thornton, a FAA preflight specialist, said he feared somebody may have pressured Wellstone's pilot to fly the senator to a funeral in northeastern Minnesota during the last days of his close re-election campaign." Wellstone had decided not to make a campaign appearance with Ted Kennedy in Maple Grove so he could go to the funeral. We have learned that Wellstone called the family on Tuesday morning announcing he would attend the funeral on Friday. This information reveals the possibility that the trip in the small plane to the small airport may have been set up somehow, or at least that many people knew about the planned trip well in advance of the flight. This would have given time and opportunity for gaining access to the plane or to make arrangements intended to cause a most unfortunate accident.

Steven Thornton was working the preflight position when the pilot of the Wellstone plane called in for a weather briefing. According to a February 4, 2002 factual NTSB report by Air Traffic Control Group Chairman, Barbara Zimmermann, one item stuck in Thornton's mind. He said he felt the caller was stressed and apprehensive. He personally was concerned that someone was putting pressure on him to take the flight. Thornton recognized the airplane call letters but did not recognize the voice of the caller. He assumed it was the pilot. Similarly, Steven Szymanski who was also on duty said he had "a funny feeling" about the briefing meeting. He said the caller sounded distant. He said he recognized the call sign of the aircraft but not the caller's voice. Since weather was actually not a serious concern, what was the source of the perceived stress? Is it possible that someone besides the pilots made one of the calls?

CRASH SITE QUESTIONS

The Very High-Frequency Omnidirectional Radio beacon, used to guide planes to the runway at the airport in Eveleth, was slightly out of true. NTSB investigators later eliminated that as a contributing factor. Airplanes landed without any problems shortly before and after the crash.

According to records, the airplane was well-maintained. The pilot, Conry, and another co-pilot flew it a day earlier to North Dakota without incident.

"There was no evidence on the controller's part or from the pilot's voice that there was any difficulty," At the NTSB, Ms. Carmody said of the last conversation between the pilot and the ground. "No reported problems. No expressed concern."

Something changed in the next 60 seconds, because at 10:19 A.M. the twin-engine aircraft began drifting slightly to the south, radar showed. The last appearance on radar came about two minutes later, as the plane was just north of the crash site's east side. "A normal landing would have continued heading straight west," Carmody said. "We find the whole turn curious." Yet, later this curiosity would be explained by NTSB and Carmody simply as "pilot error."

The angle of impact when the plane hit the ground was 30 degrees. This is an extremely steep dive and indicates that the plane was out of control. The wing flaps, which should have been fully extended for landing, were only extended to 15 degrees (a setting used for initial approach descent). On the other hand, the NTSB reported that trees were cropped by the airplane for 150 feet. Would a 30 degree dive do this?

Frank Hilldrup took over on the Monday after the Friday crash as head of the team of about 12 investigators from the National Transportation Safety. By Tuesday, they were wrapping up their work at the site. Hilldrup responded to questions about the weather and icing and told reporters that one pilot who departed from the airport at 11:30 A.M. Friday, about 50 minutes after the crash, reported a trace of icing to light icing after entering the cloud base, which was at about 1,000 feet. At the airport, local pilots expressed doubt. By this time the chief investigator should have known ice was not a factor.

Here are a few of the author's notes that Four Arrows took on February 19, 2004, approximately 2:30 P.M.:

I just had a conversation with Frank Robert Hilldrup, the lead investigator for NTSB of the crash ... I think I caught him off guard and he contradicted himself twice. I asked him why no public meeting took place on this case. He says that NTSB only has public meetings for high profile cases. When I asked him was this not a high profile, he said, well, yes, but not really. He said only in about 50% of the investigations do they have a public meeting. Then I asked him about the NTSB policy regarding not allowing other agencies to investigate without an NTSB member being present. He concurred. So then I said, well, why was the FBI on the scene? He said he could not say for sure since he took over on Monday. He said the FBI was not a part of the investigation for sure, and, in answer to my question as to why the FBI is not listed as a party to the investigation, he said that is why their name was not on the final report. (Even though Canada NTB was listed, because, he said, they played a very small role.) I said if they were not part of the investigation then why were they there? He said, well, sometimes they are there to identify bodies, and maybe they were there, "Maybe they were responding to the conspiracy theories." So of course I asked, how could there have been any "conspiracy theories" operating before the plane crashed?... This is when he said well yes there could not have been so they must have been there to, "um, well we do use police agencies to keep people away from the site... and as I said they identify bodies. Look, I have a friend who was an FBI agent on this. I'll talk to her and call you back.

On the day of the crash, Minneapolis based FBI agent Paul McCabe reported to several news reporters that about 15 agents with the bureau's evidence response team will be assisting National Transportation Safety Board investigators, yet Frank Hilldrup says they were not part of the investigation.

On April 12, 2002 The NTSB released a press advisory that said: "The National Transportation Safety Board (NTSB) announced today it will hold a public hearing on the crash of an Emery Worldwide Airlines (EWA) DC-8 cargo-jet that occurred in Sacramento. The hearing, set for May 9, 2002..." Is a cargo jet crash a "higher profile" case than the Senator's crash?

Radar tapes, according to the NTSB, indicate the plane had descended to about 400 feet and was traveling at only 85 knots near the end of its flight, yet radar shows it then turned south, dove at an unusually steep angle and crashed. Radar coverage is not consistent in the area near Eveleth airport below 2,500 feet. Most of the speculation about the airspeed and negligent stalling of the airplane depend on radar tapes during the time the plane was below this elevation.

The airplane had a stall warning horn that is generally activated at 85 knots when landing gear is down. The horn is intentionally loud, distracting and unmistakable. In simulation conditions with the King Air 100, actual stalling (when the airplanes falls as a result of too high an angle of attack) did not occur until 69 knots. This is 16 knots slower that the speed of the Wellstone aircraft reported by the last radar information.

David Francis Walpole was the staff on duty who tracked the radar and communicated with the pilots of the Wellstone airplane. During NTSB interviews, he stated that the airplane's flight path appeared normal and not out of the ordinary with good primary and secondary radar when the plane was at 3,500 feet and about 9 miles out. He also stated that he believed that 2 different members of the flight crew operated the radios during the course of the flight.

EYEWITNESS ACCOUNTS

One of the first rescuers on the scene, firefighter Erik Jankila, told reporters that once he and the others realized they weren't there on a life-saving mission, the work at the site was deliberate, in part to help answer questions for relatives. And for him, the events took on a personal tone. "I lost a family member to homicide, and I know we had tons of questions," he said. "You try to become advocates for them."

It's surprising that Jankila would compare the crash to a homicide. Two eye-witnesses, however, independently claimed to different newspapers that they heard the engines of the Wellstone plane cutting out, or going on and off, which is a phenomenon not in alignment with an aerodynamic stall.

We also have second-hand reports of someone who heard a witness say he saw a flash of light near the tail section that was reported in a number of on-line reports, but we are not taking this for granted. We know the plane mysteriously crashed while traveling in the opposite direction of an approach. We also have an eye-witness who saw "blue smoke" coming from the crashed airplane and evidence that the fuselage burned badly and the wings did not, in spite of the fact that the fuel was in the wing tanks, which had been separated from the fuselage as it went thought the trees.

From her log home less than a mile west of the wreckage, Megen Williams agonized over not calling 911 when she heard the sound she now believes was the plane on its way down. The aircraft seemed to be running normally, she said, but sounded closer than most. She didn't see which direction it was traveling, or how far it was from her home. But she remembers hearing silence after the plane passed her house, as if the engines had cut off. Within seconds, Williams said, she heard a diving noise and then an explosion. She looked out the window and saw nothing—no smoke, no fire. She assumed the blast was the usual rumbling from an Iron Range mine.

STRANGE INTERFERENCE

Co-Author Jim Fetzer published articles in Minnesota alternative newspaper *Reader Weekly* about the Wellstone death. He proposed that use of electro-magnetic pulse weaponry might have been one way that the Senator's enemies could have brought down his plane. This explanation might seem far-fetched to some already inclined to accept the official story. But it was bolstered when he received the following from John Ongaro. Mr. Ongaro was driving past the Eveleth airport on his way to the same funeral Wellstone was to attend. He wrote:

> From: John Ongaro ‹email address omitted›
>
> Subject: Wellstone Crash/ I was within a stone's throw of...

To: jfetzer@d.umn.edu

Professor-

I have both read your two stories in the Reader and also heard you on the Duke Show concerning the suspicious events surrounding Senator Wellstone's death. Although as a rule I am usually skeptical of conspiracy theories, etc, in this instance, I think you may be onto something...

The morning of Wellstone's crash, I too was on the way to the funeral of Benny Rukavina. In fact, after the funeral when we first heard about the crash and the approximate time of the crash was reported as 10:21, I immediately thought to myself, "Jeez, I was within a couple of miles of that airport (traveling north on Hwy. #53, due west of the airport) at almost that exact moment."

The reason I was sure of this, was because I arrived at the church at exactly 10:35 after picking up my mother in law who lives just two short blocks away. Having driven this route hundreds of times, I know that it is exactly 10 minutes to Virginia from the Hwy #53 & #37 (to Hibbing) intersection. The airport is just a stone's throw from this intersection. The weather, although not sunny and warm, was not freezing rain or snow either. Instead it was cloudy, hazy, with little or no wind and just above freezing. An occasional mist fell. What was happening 10,000 feet up, may have been another story, but at and near the surface there was nothing that appeared threatening in any way.

More than anything, what caused me to write you is your electromagnetic theory and how such an event could disable the plane. You see, just a few minutes prior to reaching the Hwy #53 & #37 intersection, I distinctly remember receiving a call on my cell phone. Although I have received calls on my cell phone before that have had bad reception and barely audible, this call was in a league of its own. When I answered it, what I heard sounded like a cross between a roar and a loud humming noise. The noise seemed to be oscillating and I could not make out any words being spoken. Instead, just this loud, grotesque, sometimes screeching and humming noise.

Since then, I have discovered that a friend of mine who I had tried to call earlier that morning, said he returned my call that morning and left me a message. He said his message was something like, "Another gloomy day in NE Minnesota." Little did he know how gloomy it was about to get. Strangely, I never did receive his message on my voicemail, however, and to prove my point about receiving the call will go back through my old cell phone records to see the exact time when the incoming call came in, if you think there is good reason to do so. Could an EMP type event cause this to happen to a cell phone within a few miles of the immediate area?

Finally, I am also still troubled by an email that a friend of mine sent me the week after the crash. He said that several of his coworkers who are pilots, insisted that there was no way that the plane should have burned up the way it did. They said that someone in the immediate vicinity of the incoming plane (a nearby resident, I believe) had reported to the media that they thought they had heard a loud bang, like a gunshot, just prior to the crash. My friends email said his coworkers theorized that a hunter (or sniper, if you're at all in the ballpark) could have shot the plane and that leaking fuel could have ignited an engine. My friends coworkers said that, otherwise, it is unheard of for other plane crashes of this type of small plane to have a fire incident like this one connected with it.

Knowing Congressman Oberstar quite well, I decided to forward my email onto his Duluth office. Ironically, they emailed me back with a message that stated that the FBI had already informed them that they had already investigated any possibility of foul play and had ruled it out.

Hmmm...I wonder if it was one of their "early arriving agents?"

If you think there is any reason to further look into either of these two strange occurrences that I have presented you, please feel free to contact me.

John Ongaro

At Jim's request, John checked his cell phone records and determined that the call had come at 10:18 AM.

The remarks from his coworkers about the crash are interesting, but his experience with Congressman Oberstar, whom he knows personally, are disconcerting. More than two months later, John was still troubled. He sent Jim another email March 16, 2003, wondering to the odds that two major Democratic candidates for Senate would get killed in plane crashes in the final 10 days of a neck and neck election within two years of each other. He also referred to an NPR article on EMP weaponry.

Lawrence Judd, an Illinois attorney, later wrote the NTSB to ask whether it either has or would investigate the possibility that EMP weapons were used to bring down the planes of Senators Wellstone and Carnahan. Robert Benzon, the same person on the scene who reported that the NTSB was searching for signs that icing brought down the plane, wrote him back, thusly: "The NTSB is unaware of any mobile EM force or EM pulse weapon system capable of disabling an aircraft at the ground-to-air ranges that existed in either of the accidents you mention in your email."

It seems impossible that the NTSB would not know about such weapons. As we explain in Chapter Seven, these weapons do exist and they can bring down planes. In fact, that's what they were designed for.

CRASH SCENE WRECKAGE

At 11:35, KSTP, Channel 5, was given a tip about a plane crash from its sister station in Duluth, WDIO-TV. Around noon, Bob McNaney, informally the station's aviation reporter, called Wellstone's campaign office. The tone of the voice on the other end of the line tipped him that Wellstone's people were concerned. The senator's party should have landed an hour earlier, but no one had heard anything. At 12:10 P.M., the first, formal confirmation of the crash came in from the FAA, with the plane's tail number, which was matched to the plane leased to the Wellstone campaign. Rob Hubbard, president of the Hubbard Television Group, gave the local station the company jet to immediately fly a crew north. Thirty-seven minutes after wheels up, the five were on the ground in Hibbing (the closest airport to the crash that could handle a jet), and jumping into prearranged rental cars heading for the Eveleth airport. KSTP also had two satellite trucks on the road north, in addition to another satellite rig from WDIO. The reporters were at the airport 90 minutes from the time they first received the news. It was more than 8 hours before any members of the NTSB team arrived. Rescue workers reported that the tail and wings were separated from the fuselage.

The post-crash fire consumed the cockpit and fuselage and the only recognizable parts remaining were the tail and part of the wings. "It looks like a tremendous fire pit," said Kevin Smith, a spokesman for the Minnesota Department of Public Safety. The fuselage, which was separated from the wings that contained the fuel tank, burned for hours emitting blue smoke. The type of fuel in this plane should have emitted a thick, black smoke. Why was the fuselage burning rather than the wings, especially when the wings were found separated from the fuselage? Blue smoke generally means an electrical fire.

In response to a question about whether the fuselage would burn to a mechanic who specializes in this particular aircraft, Four Arrows received the following reply:

> Dr. Jacobs,
>
> The King Air A100 carries it's fuel in only the wings. Only minor plumbing is in the fuselage. This is so either wing can feed fuel to either engine. I do not believe the fuselage would catch fire. As to the color of the smoke, I have no idea.
>
> I hope this helps you.
>
> Best regards,
>
> Ken Haley, Service Manager, Cutter Aviation

In his article, "Wellstone and 9/11: The Uncanny Connections", Christopher Bollyn of the *American Free Press* reported that agents from the FBI's Minneapolis Evidence Response Team have been accused of stealing evidence from the site of the World Trade Center, where they had been sent to investigate. The stolen evidence was a valuable Tiffany crystal paperweight taken from a WTC evidence bag. Perhaps readers might think nothing of the theft of a trinket, but the incident is telling. This grave-robbing exposes the FBI's disregard for the memory of the 9/11 victims and it shows a culture of abuse at the FBI. This is a branch of law enforcement that from its behavior seems to believe it can do as it pleases. It is no stretch to infer that an agency that would steal valuables from the WTC is capable of cleaning up a crash scene to remove incriminating evidence. There had to have been powerful reasons for getting the team to the crash site so quickly that it even risked exposing its role in a cover up.

In an odd connection to the 9/11 disaster, Bollyn also reported that the co-pilot who flew with Wellstone had known Zacharias Moussaoui, the accused conspirator who had attended the Eagan (MN) flight school. Co-pilot Michael Guess, 30, had met the flying student Moussaoui at the Pan Am International Flight Academy where Guess worked last year (2001). Guess had reportedly "inadvertently" given Moussaoui unattended access to a computer program on flying a 747 jumbo jet. An ex-manager of Pan Am told the FBI that Guess had placed a CD-ROM containing the 747 software at a workstation before one of Moussaoui's training sessions. After Moussaoui was arrested, the FBI searched his belongings and found the proprietary program copied on his laptop computer, the ex-manager said. Guess had recently been laid off at the flight academy, where he had hoped to become a flight instructor.

"At Executive Aviation in Eden Prairie, where Guess had been employed as a pilot since June 2001, a spokesman said colleagues remembered Guess telling them he had played a more significant role regarding the suspicions concerning Moussaoui," the *Star Tribune* reported.

Dave Mona, a spokesman for Executive Aviation, said Guess's colleagues had said Guess had described himself as "at least a role player" in the detection of Moussaoui. Mona said Guess had told his colleagues that "he and the receptionist...thought what [Moussaoui] was requesting was unusual" and had raised the issue with others.

(see www.americanfreepress.net)

Although not required on this airplane, Bill Wilkerson, who has been hiring pilots and leasing small planes for more than 30 years, points out in a posting on the NPR web site that A100s have the best avionics in the business and usually also carry black boxes because of the calibre of their customer. NTSB's field leader, Carol Carmody, said early on she was looking for the black box and reported this to numerous newspapers the day of the crash. FAA spokesman Paul Takemoto stated in several reports that the plane should have been equipped with a flight data recorder (black box) and a cockpit voice recorder. No such equipment was ever found, and later Carmody said that thinking this plane had one had been a mistake.

According to Tony Kennedy and Greg Gordon of the *Star Tribune,* a former investigator for the National Transportation Safety Board (NTSB) said the ongoing probe into the plane crash that killed Paul Wellstone includes an unusually strong focus on the qualifications of the two pilots. "It makes you wonder how it will be worked in when the board determines probable cause," said Chuck Leonard, a retired senior investigator who worked on more than 200 NTSB investigations.

William A. Shields, a *USA Daily* columnist, an ex-Marine with 19 years experience as an air traffic controller and a past president of the National Air Traffic Controllers Association, EWR Local, he has held positions in the rail, aviation and marine transportation industries. He wrote an article entitled, "Support Your Local Whistleblower," in which he gave a number of examples of NTSB official positions being totally inappropriate. Shields described the NTSB's power to make life uncomfortable for any employee who challenges such conclusions.

FAA spokesman Les Dorr said FAA agency officials are curious about the criticism that NTSB levied that they should have conducted en route inspections of flight operations at Eveleth because Aviation Charter last year received the second highest number of inspections of any carrier overseen by the agencies, according to the Minneapolis Flight Standards District Office.

"They were no longer in control of the aircraft." Said Don Sipola, a former president of the Eveleth Virginia Municipal Airport Commission, who has 25 years of experience flying at the airport. "That will be the $64 question—what occurred in the last few minutes that distracted them or caused them to wrestle control of the aircraft. Something caused them at low altitude to veer off course."

Precisely what that "something" may have been has generated a variety of answers, some of which are painful to confront. Because if the plane was not brought down by the weather, the pilots, or the plane, then we are compelled to consider the prospect that this was no accident.

PRECEDENTS FOR ASSASSINATION

According to an article by Michael Ruppert in his on-line news journal, *From the Wilderness*, and other sources, Paul Wellstone had been a target of harassment from official channels at least once before. He was strident opponent of Plan Colombia, a U.S. military aid package which involves massive aerial spraying of lands believed to be growing cocaine and the use of private military contractors employed by companies like DynCorp. Wellstone had traveled to Colombia to evaluate the program. Shortly after his arrival on December 1, 2000, as reported by multiple news sources, a bomb was found along his route from the airport. Although the State Department later downplayed the incident, the general opinion was, and remains, that as an outspoken critic of CIA and covert operations, Wellstone had indeed been a target.

Those suspicions gained credibility the next day when Wellstone and his staff were sprayed with glyphosate, a chemical that has been routinely documented as the cause of a variety of illnesses in the local population. It has left certain regions of Colombia, as one native put it, "Without butterflies or birds."

One anonymous author, using the pen name Vox Fux, actually predicted Wellstone's assassination in spring 2001. The story can be read at www.voxnyc.com. In that missive the author predicted, "If the death occurs just prior to the midterm senatorial elections, expect it to be in a state with a close race. Expect a 'Mel Carnahan' style hit."

Shortly after writing this uncanny prediction, Vox Fux published a satirical article on his website that responded to the Bush White House's recent approval of instant CIA assassinations against any U.S. or other citizens with suspected ties to Al Qaeda. Vox Fux pointed out that Bush himself had done business with Al Qaeda's Osama Bin Laden and therefore should be "Immediately Terminated...No Trial, No Explanation, No Warning." Vox Fux's website headquarters was raided by Secret Service and the local police's Special Crimes unit within days. (Our editor, Sander Hicks, happened to write a feature article on this raid on Vox Fux's home for the New York City-area weekly *Long Island Press* at the time.)

see: http://sanderhicks.com/archives.html

CHAPTER FOUR

ASSASSINATION SCIENCE

I am convinced the FBI, in developing its report, failed to give sufficient weight to the considerable harassment, intimidation, and death
threats Father Kaiser faced as he challenged officials of the Moi regime.

—Senator Paul Wellstone
Referring to the FBI's conclusion
that civil rights activist
John Kaiser committed suicide.

FROM SPECULATION TO RIGOR

The 1960's comedian, Flip Wilson, had a routine where he
explained his outrageous behavior by saying, *"The Devil made me do
it!"* This phrase soon became a fun, household phrase. The reason for
its popularity is that *"The Devil made me do it"* is an untestable
assertion. It could be invoked to explain earthquakes, hurricanes, or
other disasters, but no one can show that it is false. The Devil might,
after all, be luring us into a false sense of security by making things
come out right for a change, only to make our later suffering all the
more painful. So good things, as well as bad, can be reconciled with
the "devil hypothesis", making it untestable.

A certain unclarity derives from confusion about the meaning of
"theory." There's a distinction between "theories" in the ordinary
sense: mere speculations or conjectures, supposedly unsupported by
evidence (as when it is said, "Oh, that's just a theory") as opposed to
"theories" in the scientific sense, as speculations or conjectures that
are capable of rigorous development and empirical test, such as
Newton's theory of gravitation and Einstein's theory of relativity.

They have mathematical structure and have been repeatedly subjected to tests based upon the observations, measurements, and experiments, which have falsified Newton while confirming Einstein. These have been among the most important developments in the history of science. What becomes important in thinking about alternatives is sorting out those that are merely speculative from those that are serious and subject to test.

One of the problems in looking beyond the official explanation of the Wellstone crash is that the "devil hypothesis" can be applied to innumerable scenarios. The hypothesis that Senator Paul Wellstone was assassinated as the result of a conspiracy is somewhere in between "theories" that are merely speculations and "theories" that are subjected to rigorous development and empirical test. The point of our book might be appropriately described as that of taking the assassination hypothesis from the domain of "mere speculation" and subjecting it to the rigorous development and empirical test that its serious study requires. The stages of inquiry that are involved here are the same stages that are fundamental to scientific investigations in general, namely: puzzlement, speculation, adaptation, and explanation.

The stage of puzzlement occurs when something turns out to be the case that invites further study, usually because it does not accord with our previously existing knowledge and beliefs. The Wellstone crash would not have been puzzling but for the circumstances surrounding the event we have described. The stage of speculation occurs when an attempt is made to elaborate all of the alternative explanations that are physically possible. This stage is quite important, because much of scientific inquiry involves the elimination of alternatives that are inconsistent with the available evidence. If an hypothesis has not been included in the set of alternatives, it cannot possibly emerge as the most likely explanation for the phenomenon that concerns us—whether it is the fall of an apple from a tree, the paths of the planets around the sun, or the crash of a King Air A-100 in Minnesota —even when it happens to be true. Just viewing the matter purely hypothetically relative to the alternatives "accident" or "assassination", if an investigation focuses solely upon one, such as accident, and excludes the other altogether, then it should come as no surprise when its "conclusion" turns out to be that it was an accident.

The stage of adaptation involves evaluating alternatives on the basis of the available relevant evidence. Evidence is relevant when its presence or absence (truth or falsity) makes a difference to the truth or falsity of one or more of the hypotheses under consideration. It "makes a difference" when its presence or absence (truth or falsity) increases or decreases the likelihood of an hypothesis, where the likelihood of an hypothesis equals the probability of the evidence, if it were true. Where we designate "accident" as (h1) and "assassination" as (h2), and the available relevant evidence by "(e)", then (h1) "accident" is preferable to (h2) "assassination" when the probability of the evidence (e), given the accident hypothesis, (h1), is greater than the probability of the evidence (e), given the assassination hypothesis, (h2). Under these conditions, the likelihood of (h1) accident is greater than the likelihood of (h2) assassination, relative to (e).

What this would mean is that the accident hypothesis, (h1), provides a better explanation than the assassination hypothesis, (h2), given the available evidence, (e). That would be the case if (h1) makes (e) more probable than does (h2). When one hypothesis provides a better explanation of the available evidence than does another, the first is preferable to the second. When one hypothesis provides a better explanation of the available evidence than any other, then it is preferable to any other. When the available evidence is sufficient, which occurs when it has "settled down", then the preferable hypothesis also becomes acceptable. If none of the alternative hypotheses is reasonable, moreover, then its acceptance may be appropriately described as having been established "beyond a reasonable doubt". But reaching this point requires taking into account all of the available relevant evidence and presupposes that all of the alternative hypotheses are considered.

From a logical point of view, the most conspicuous inadequacy of the NTSB's investigation of the death of Paul Wellstone is that it only considered variations on the accident hypothesis. It never took assassination as a genuine alternative or investigated the possible use of a small bomb, a gas canister or EMP weaponry. The NTSB had the FBI's assertion that no terrorist activity had been involved, but we have seen that the FBI's involvement raises troublesome questions.

The term, "terrorist", is extremely vague and could obscure a rather broad range of criminal activities. Moreover, the evidence which the NTSB considered does not appear to have been complete. There are various ways in which evidence can be relevant but not available or available but not relevant. Of the multiple ways in which the true causes of a crime can be concealed, none is more powerful than making sure that the available evidence has been selected—or even created—to support the "official" depiction of the crime. The simplest is to exclude the true hypothesis.

THE DEATH OF JFK

The Columbia Space Shuttle disaster investigation violated scientific reasoning by excluding relevant hypotheses from consideration and by ignoring important, potentially crucial, photographic evidence. (For more on the strange anomalies that might have brought down the Columbia, see Jim Fetzer's website at *assassinationscience.com*) These techniques, especially the exclusion of relevant hypotheses, have been fundamental to the cover up in the case of Senator Paul Wellstone.

The domain of "assassination science", however, offers even more stunning examples of improprieties, especially the cover up in the case of President John F. Kennedy. The investigation in this case violated scientific reasoning in ways that are both more blatant and more subtle. More blatant by taking for granted that the alleged assassin committed the crime; more subtle, by altering, suppressing, and manufacturing evidence in order to frame him. All three cases display the influence of politics in trumping science.

Any American who wants to understand how the American government misleads the American people must appreciate the full range and extent of the measures that are employed for that purpose. The death of a United States Senator that concerns us is but a single instance in a pattern of deceit and deception that has been used time and again to deprive the American people of the truth about their own history. If we are to cope with cases of this kind, then we need a real education about how these things are done, where there could be no more instructive illustration than the death of a United States President in which virtually all the "tricks of the trade" were employed. Understanding how it was done in this historic case allows us to better understand how it is still being done today, including the case that concerns us. We must learn from the past if we are to end being misled in the future by agencies of our own government.

According to *The Warren Report* (1964), *The House Select Committee's Final Report* (1979), and Gerald Posner's *Case Closed* (1993), among others, President John F. Kennedy was killed by two shots, one of which hit the base of the back of his neck, transited his neck without hitting any bony structures, and exited his throat just above his tie before entering the back of Texas Governor John Connally to the left of his right armpit, passing through his chest after shattering a rib, and exiting near his right nipple, impacting with his right wrist and finally lodging in his left thigh—a bullet that the government claims to have recovered which has only modest longitudinal distortion. (It is widely known as the "magic" bullet.) A second shot hit him in the back of his head and killed him, while a third shot—perhaps the first fired—missed and injured a distant bystander, James Tague.

The evidence in this case has always been fraught with controversy, where some 40 eyewitnesses—at Dealey Plaza where the shooting occurred, Parkland Hospital, where he was initially treated, and Bethesda Naval Hospital, where the body was taken for autopsy—reported a massive blow-out to the back of his head. But the eyewitnesses were dismissed on the ground that the X-rays taken at the autopsy do not show a defect of this kind. More than 60 witnesses reported having observed the Presidential limousine either slow dramatically or come to a complete halt in Dealey Plaza after bullets began to be fired, reports that were discounted on the basis that photos and films taken at the time of the assassination did not show it. And there was inconsistent evidence as to whether Lee Oswald, the alleged assassin, had even been on the 6th floor of the Texas Book Depository Building, which was the alleged site of the purported "assassin's lair".

The "magic bullet" theory was a fabrication from scratch. Holes in the shirt and the jacket he was wearing are about 5 1/2 inches below the collar. While some argue that they were tugged upward at the time, that would not explain an autopsy diagram showing a wound at the same location by a medical officer assisting in the procedure nor another by an FBI observer showing the wound to the back lower than the wound to the throat. The death certificate executed by the President's personal physician describes the wound at the level of the third thoracic vertebra, which is about 5 1/2 inches below the collar. The mortician's description of the body includes a small wound of entry to the right temple, a massive blow-out to the back of the head, and a wound to the back about 5-6 inches below the collar. The evidence clearly refutes the "magic bullet" theory.

Even the Warren Commission staff initially took for granted that the wound to the back was well below the collar, as reenactment photographs reflect. One of them even shows Arlen Specter with a pointer showing the trajectory that the "magic bullet" had to have taken, while below his hand you can see a patch that was being used to mark the wounds. So a photograph that was intended to illustrate the theory actually refutes it. It turns out that Michigan Congressman Gerald Ford had the wound's description changed to "the base of the back of the neck" from "the uppermost back", which was already an exaggeration, to make the "magic bullet" theory more plausible. David W. Mantik, M.D., Ph.D., has now proven that the official trajectory is not even anatomically possible by taking a patient with similar neck dimensions and charting the path that it would have taken, which is physically impossible because cervical vertebrae intervene.

JFK had a wound to his throat caused by a shot from the front that even passed through the limousine windshield en route to its target. He had another wound to his back about 5 1/2 inches below the collar, which was a shallow injury that only penetrated about as far as the second knuckle of your little finger. He had two shots to the head, one to the back of the head from behind, the other entering the right temple, a frangible (or "exploding") bullet with shock waves that blew his brains out the back of his head. Connally's wounds, therefore, had to have been caused by other shots and other shooters. Michael Baden, M.D., who chaired the panel that reviewed medical records for the House Select Committee when it reinvestigated the case in 1977-78, recently remarked that, if the "magic bullet" theory is false, then there had to have been at least six shots from at least three different directions.

When the authentic evidence has been separated from the inauthentic, then it becomes straightforward to draw an inference to the best explanation. While the Mafia (or the CIA) could have put up some of the shooter to take JFK out, it could not have extended its reach into Bethesda Naval Hospital to alter X-rays that were under the control of the Secret Service, U.S. Navy medical officers, and the President's personal physician. Neither pro nor anti-Castro Cubans could have substituted another brain for that of JFK. The Soviet KGB, which would have had the same ability to subject a home movie of the assassination to sophisticated alteration, would have had no opportunity to gain its possession. Nor could any of these things have been done by Lee Oswald, who was incarcerated or already dead.

Only certain factions or privileged individuals with the authority of the U.S. government had the ability to change the evidence, which "it" would have done in order to conceal its complicity in committing the crime. In the same fashion that there is obvious involvement of the FBI and Capitol Police in the Wellstone investigation, more than forty years of research into the death of JFK provides extensive support for the hypothesis that the Secret Service set up the President for the hit, that the CIA/Military/Mafia took him out, that the FBI covered it up, with direction from LBJ and J. Edgar Hoover and the complicity of Allen Dulles, with financing from wealthy Texas oil men, all of whom had powerful reasons for wanting to displace the political policies of JFK with the political policies of LBJ.

THE DEATH OF DAVID KELLY

Many other cases help illustrate the methods and mistakes of thinking associated with Paul Wellstone's death. The death of British scientist David Kelly is notable for its timeliness, for its glaring and obvious deception and governmental cover-up, and for its relationship to the events surrounding the war in Iraq. Kelly's science contradicted the claims by George Bush and others about weapons of mass destruction, an issue about which Paul Wellstone posed another threat to the U.S. administration's credibility. This case should likewise disturb not merely every American but every resident of the world who cares about exposing corruption.

Just as it was assumed that Senator Wellstone's airplane crash was an accident from the beginning in spite of obvious possibilities to the contrary, the inquiry into the death of David Kelly took for granted his death was suicide. After Dr. Kelly "went for a walk" in the English countryside on July 17, 2003, he was found dead. His wrists were slashed, and the official verdict was suicide. Yet, reports stated Kelly's mental state was buoyant, and his apparent happiness makes suicide unlikely. Further details on exactly how his wrists were cut, the position of his body, the low amount of bleeding, and the pills found at the scene add up to a preposterous official story. Kelly's death had clear political advantages. He died just prior to his official testimony that would have discredited the Iraq invasion justifications of Bush and Blair. Nonetheless, the official conclusions has gone largely unchallenged.

Kelly was a member of the UN inspection team in Iraq looking for "weapons of mass destruction." In an e-mail sent the morning of his death, he warned of "many dark actors playing games." *The New York Times* reported that the message referred to the British Ministry of Defense, and intelligence agencies, with whom Kelly had sparred. A recently retired senior British Intelligence officer a Lieutenant Colonel Crispin Black, described the government's Hutton Report on Kelly's death as a "laughing stock."

CONSPIRACY THEORIES

A "conspiracy" only requires two or more persons acting together to bring about an illegal end. It would be absurd to dismiss the possibility that puzzling events with profound economic and political consequences might not have resulted from conspiracies. To dismiss discoveries like those we have presented above on the grounds that they should be ignored because, no matter how detailed and elaborate may be their supporting evidence, they are unacceptable, in principle, appears to be a nice example of the ostrich policy. Indeed, fostering such an attitude appears to be a classic example of the use of propaganda to inhibit "sane" persons from taking them seriously. When the evidence is there, what kind of "sanity" is this?

In his study, "'Conspiracy Theories' and Clandestine Politics" for LOBSTER.com, Jeffrey M. Bale makes the case that the very idea of conspiracies tends to send shivers down the backs of respectable academics and of others who envision themselves as intellectually sophisticated. Bale captures this attitude perfectly (http://www.mindcontrol-forums.com/conspiracy-theories.htm) in the following:

AMERICAN ASSASSINATION

> *Very few notions generate as much intellectual resistance, hostility, and derision within academic circles as a belief in the historical importance or efficacy of political conspiracies. Even when this belief is expressed in a very cautious manner, limited to specific and restricted contexts, supported by reliable evidence, and hedged about with all sort of qualifications, it still manages to transcend the boundaries of acceptable discourse and violate unspoken academic taboos. The idea that particular groups of people meet together secretly or in private to plan various courses of action, and that some of these plans actually exert a significant influence on particular historical developments, is typically rejected out of hand and assumed to be the figment of a paranoid imagination.*

As university professors ourselves, we know that Bale has hit the nail on the head:

> *The mere mention of the word "conspiracy" seems to set off an internal alarm bell which causes scholars to close their minds in order to avoid cognitive dissonance and possible unpleasantness, since the popular image of conspiracy both fundamentally challenges the conception most educated, sophisticated people have about how the world operates and reminds them of the horrible persecutions that absurd and unfounded conspiracy theories have precipitated or sustained in the past. So strong is this prejudice among academics that even when clear evidence of a plot is inadvertently discovered in the course of their own research, they frequently feel compelled, either out of a sense of embarrassment or a desire to defuse anticipated criticism, to preface their account of it by ostentatiously disclaiming a belief in conspiracies.*

We are both acquainted with colleagues and acquaintances who realize this conception to its highest exemplification. To those knowledgeable about the death of JFK, some of the most acute disappointments of their lives have revolved about denial by prominent intellectuals, such as Noam Chomsky, who has made a point of debunking "high level" conspiracy theories about the death of JFK as a form of romanticism that has no place in the minds of serious scholars. But it is difficult to reconcile such a posture with altered X-rays, a substitute brain, faking the film, and framing a patsy for the crime, all proven beyond a reasonable doubt.

Some academics are so powerfully affected by their commitment to an anti-conspiracy mindset they even seem to lose temporary control of their rationality. They feel compelled to deny the very possibility of plots and refuse to consider contrary evidence as a matter of ideology independent of experience. Each case has to be investigated on its own merits.

Noam Chomsky is a celebrated scholar and icon of the political left. Arguably the most influential critical intellectual alive today, he is also a respected friend and colleague of Four Arrows. Many of Chomsky's followers and champions were confused when he dismissed the possibility that power elites of the U.S. government might have assassinated JFK:

> *It's true that I know very little about the assassination. The only thing I've written about it is that the claim that it was a high-level conspiracy with policy significance is implausible to a quite extraordinary degree. History isn't physics, and even in physics nothing is really "proven," but the evidence against this claim is overwhelming, from every testable point of view, remarkably so for a historical event. Given that conclusion, which I think is very well founded (that I have written about, a lot), I have no further interest in the assassination, and while I've read a few of the books, out of curiosity, I haven't given the matter any attention and have no opinion about how or why JFK was killed.*
>
> *People shouldn't be killed, whether they are presidents or kids in the urban slums. I know of no reason to suppose that one should have more interest in the JFK assassination than lots of killings not far from the White House. As for whether "power elites perceived JFK to be a threat to the status quo," the statement is close to meaningless. If someone can produce some coherent version of the statement, and then some evidence for that version, I'll be glad to look at it.*
>
> *(The text is at http://www.zmag.org/forums/chomskyforumcmt.htm)*

Chomsky is not denying that JFK might have been taken out as the result of a conspiracy but asserting that he has no evidence of a "high level" conspiracy. He admits that he knows "very little" about the case, which is significant, since it is rather difficult to imagine how the autopsy X-rays could have been altered (or another brain substituted or the Zapruder film been recreated or the patsy have been framed using manufactured evidence) in the absence of a "high level" conspiracy. His lack of interest, however, appears to be anchored in a lack of awareness of the major policy implications of the assassination. If a man of his stature could so clearly misread recent American history, then it becomes all the more understandable why many other Americans, especially within the academic community, might be reluctant to come to grips with the grim reality of the death of JFK.

Thus, even though the authors' disagree with Chomsky's conclusion about the JFK assassination not being a high-level policy decision, we did not bring him up to argue this complicated subject. Rather, we want to make two points. First, even our "left wing" associates, those as committed to critical thinking as Chomsky, may be influenced by the strong stigma against "conspiracy theorist." Second, the main arguments Chomsky and others have against the JFK assassination being a high level conspiracy support the claim that Wellstone was assassinated as part of a high level policy decision. That is, Chomsky does not believe JFK was assassinated by high level policy makers because he claims that Kennedy was in bed with these decision makers. This is certainly not the case with Wellstone, yet Noam and others like him are unwilling to use their same argument to look at the Wellstone case as a high level conspiracy.

In his best-selling book, *Against All Enemies* (2004), Richard Clarke has a few things to say that are also relevant to "conspiracy theories." Since Clark was the highest level person in counter-terrorism for the past three presidents, his words are worth heeding. Clark is skeptical also of conspiracy theories in general. He says that a problem with them is that the theorists generally hold two opposing views simultaneously—one that the government is too incompetent to discover what the theorists have discovered, but are so competent that they can keep great secrets about it. In the Wellstone case, like in many successful murder plots, we agree about the incompetence of government agencies, but hold that only a very few highly selected individuals know the secret and realize the cost of revealing it.

But we also agree with *four* other points Clarke makes in his book. First, he says that Vice President Cheney is the most right-wing ideologue in a high-ranking position he has ever seen. Second, he says that the Bush Administration's secrecy is equal to the mafia's. Third, he says, "It is dangerous to dismiss conspiracy theories out of hand."(!) Finally, Clarke refers to the covert assassination policy of our government for taking out known terrorists. Could it be that

Cheney's fanatical extremism, combined with his personal hatred of Wellstone (Cheney was barred from attending the Wellstone's funeral, let's not forget) might have brought him to see Wellstone as equal to a terrorist in the way of Cheney's own "patriotic" duty and acted accordingly?

In his book, *Dirty Truths* (1996), Michael Parenti properly challenges Noam's position with this astute observation: "Chomsky is able to maintain his criticism that no credible evidence has come to light only by remaining determinedly unacquainted with the mountain of evidence that has been uncovered." He has acknowledged as much in the passage we quote. Indeed, it is probably fair to speculate that his resistance to looking at the evidence has at least two roots:

First, the scope of his research in many areas, including but not limited to linguistic theory, is already admirable and his contributions to the critique of U.S. domestic and foreign policies are remarkable. Perhaps we can explain his decision not to expend his own energy researching who killed JFK on that basis.

Second, the most popular argument for why government forces might have assassinated JFK is that he was planning on withdrawing from Viet Nam without victory, something not to be tolerated by powerful forces benefiting from the war, where the CIA wanted him out for how he mishandled the Bay of Pigs. Chomsky has written an entire book rebutting these ideas (*Rethinking Camelot*, 1993).

However unfortunate, it would thus seem to be a natural response for him to dismiss the conspiracy theory in general, whether or not he is correct, and many think he is not. In his recent autobiographical movie, "Fog of War", even Robert McNamara said that he thought Kennedy would have pulled the troops out, and Parenti has ample resources that conflict with his position on the CIA with regard to JFK.

The differences between JFK's and LBJ's policy toward Vietnam, moreover, is only one of many profound differences between them, including cutting the oil depletion allowance, reforming or abolishing the Federal Reserve, and shattering the CIA into a thousand pieces. He had offended the Joint Chiefs by not invading Cuba (against their unanimous recommendation) and by signing an above ground test-ban treaty with the Soviet Union (against their unanimous opposition). He was dropping LBJ as his running mate for 1964 and was going to retire J. Edgar Hoover as Director of the FBI after his reelection. Many on the right feared that Bobby would succeed Jack and Teddy would succeed Bobby, creating a Kennedy dynasty that would entrench broadly liberal policies forever.

POISONOUS PRECEDENTS

There are many other mysterious deaths within the United States that appear to be related to corporate or political intrigue but are explained away as "accidents." Some of them may initially appear to be accidental or coincidental, yet as new evidence emerges, the incidents appear increasingly puzzling. When political considerations are factored in, certain historical incidents become even more of a possible precedent for criminality, especially when the past incidents involve the Bush administration.

Marvin Bush, the youngest of the President's brothers, was recently involved in a disturbing incident. On October 5, 2003, *The Washington Post* ran a small story with the headline, "Bush Family Babysitter Killed in Fairfax." It described the death of family babysitter Bertha Champagne in a freakish automobile accident:

> A babysitter for the family of Marvin Bush was found dead Monday night outside the family's Fairfax County home, and police said that she had been crushed when her car rolled into her, pinning her between the vehicle and an outbuilding on the property.

> Fairfax County police said Bertha Champagne, 62, had worked for several years for Marvin Bush, President Bush's brother, and lived at the family home on Fort Hunt Road in the Alexandria section of Fairfax.

> Officer Courtney Young, a police spokeswoman, said Champagne had gone outside the house about 9 p.m. Monday, reportedly to retrieve something from her car. The vehicle had been in gear, police said, and appeared to have rolled in her direction when Champagne was in front of it.

> After pinning Champagne, Young said, the car continued rolling toward Fort Hunt Road, near the intersection of Edgehill Drive. Champagne was taken to an area hospital and declared dead that evening. Young said she did not know the cause of death.

In this case, a cause of death this improbable surely deserves a homicide investigator. It is a distinct possibility, that the 62-year-old woman, who had been with the family for "several years", might have come to possess information that Bush would have found embarrassing, or incriminating. It is not difficult to combine possible motive with means and opportunity, especially given the strange sequence of events. How could a car, in gear without a driver, pin Ms. Champagne against a building, crush her to death, and then continue rolling across a busy street, only to land safely in a wooded area?

Throughout this book we are sifting through facts, mysterious connections, historical perspectives, and questionable practices. These have lead us the shocking possibility, no, probability, that the oily leadership of the United States of America, led by the Bush-Cheney gang, assassinated one of the last of America's political leaders. There was a multi-billion dollar motivation and a sloppy cover-up with an apparent "no-questions asked" mandate.

We are weaving information about the assassination of John F. Kennedy into our inquiry, not only to show similarities in investigative cover-ups but to hint at a history of the Bush-Cheney legacy too few are willing to address. Let's take a moment and explore that legacy.

When John Hinckley, Jr. nearly assassinated Ronald Reagan, Hinckley was dismissed as a "lone nut." However, the Hinckley and Bush families have a long history together back in Midland, Texas. John's brother, Scott, was scheduled to have dinner in Denver at the home of Neil Bush, George W. Bush's brother, the very evening of the attempt on Reagan (a fact reported by *Newsweek* and NBC). Neil Bush worked for Standard Oil, and Scott Hinckley for Vanderbilt Energy Corporation. George Herbert Walker Bush, former Director of the CIA, was Reagan's Vice-President after losing the presidential nomination to Reagan in a fierce primary campaign. President Bush would have become President before 1989 had Reagan been incapacitated from serving. A great deal about Neil Bush and the family can be learned from Peter Brewton, *The Mafia, CIA and George Bush* (1992).

Although the assassination attempt failed to catapult Bush into the White House early, it might have attained its desired results. It may have scared the conservative ex-actor into submission to the extreme tactics of the Bush-Cheney crew. John Hinckley, Sr., a major to Bush campaign contributor, was arrested in 1980 at an airport where

Jimmy Carter was arriving, for possessing a .38 caliber pistol, two .22 caliber handguns and 50 rounds of ammunition. His son John Hinckley, Jr. participated in a Christian Evangelical organization called "World Vision," an entity that served as a refugee charity and recruiting station for U.S. intelligence in Vietnam and other troubled regions.

One of the more striking developments has come from an unexpected source. Our editor, Sander Hicks, and co-writer, Toby Rogers, made some important discoveries on links between Bush, and the JFK assassination. They wrote an obituary for Richard Helms, former director of the CIA, for a major Japanese newspaper. The piece included an interview with a "Mr. Fly" a former officer of the Office of Strategic Services, (precursor to the CIA) who knew enough to be able to plan on and attend the assassination in Dallas. That evening the former officer saw Bush at parties arranged by Republicans:

> There were three pre-planned, post-hit parties in Dallas at private homes of wealthy Texas Mafia the night Kennedy was taken out. "You have to remember, November 22, 1963 was a Friday. All the 'big boys' in Oil were there along with CIA people." Fly went to one at a silver tycoon's mansion, and saw future President (and future CIA Director) George H.W. Bush there. "But I believe he was torn, like many others in the room. I mean think about it, the President of the United States was just murdered and here they were sipping champagne like it was New Year's Eve. It was a very creepy, surreal atmosphere that still haunts me to this day."
> (See Toby Rogers, Ambushed: Secrets of the Bush Family, the Stolen Presidency, 9/11, and 2004 (2004).)

Although the official story is that Bush, Sr., was never a member of the CIA until he was appointed its Director, there are ample indications that this is not the case. His history with the agency was extensive: Earlier in his administration, Kennedy called off the Bay of Pigs invasion of Cuba using right-wing Cuban emigres. The code name for the Bay of Pigs operation was "Zapata", which was the name of the Bush family's oil-drilling company. Two of the ships were rechristened, one renamed "Barbara", and the other "Houston", just before the abortive mission. (See "Bush, George Herbert Walker", in Michael Benson's *Encyclopedia of the JFK Assassination* (2002)).

These are precedents of which few Americans are aware. There is an active disinformation operation when it comes to JFK, the objective of which is to make everything believable and nothing knowable, as Martin Schotz put it in *History Will Not Absolve Us* (1996). We have already recounted evidence of a disinformation campaign regarding the death of the courageous Senator from Minnesota. For these and other reasons elaborated in this book, we believe that the Bush administration, including Cheney, Rove, and Rumsfeld, would not have hesitated in taking him out. The stakes were high and their cause, to them, was just. The vast majority of Americans however, would be appalled to learn the bitter truth.

DISCREDITING THE DEBUNKERS

Several books have also been written that contribute to the negative image of anyone who truly would employ "assassination science" to investigate assassinations or explore the possible existence of conspiracies. One such publication announces its attitude on its cover. *Kooks: A Guide To The Outer Limits Human Belief* (1994). Another that attacks those who advance conspiracy theories to explain otherwise inexplicable things is *Conspiracy Theories: Secrecy And Power In American Culture* (2001). Its author, Mark Fenster, believes that conspiracy theories have become a source of thrills for a bored subculture, one epitomized by its members' reinterpretation of "accepted" history, deep cynicism about contemporary politics, and longing for some utopian future. However much these words may describe fans of "The X-Files", they are inconsistent with objective and scientific research on the death of JFK that establishes the existence of a conspiracy and cover-up.

Another such book by Timothy Melly, *Empire Of Conspiracy: The Culture Of Paranoia In Postwar America* (2000), offers a more academic approach. Like the many "scholarly" books being published that depict the worldviews and accomplishments of Native Americans as "useless", it promotes the dismissal of American Indian worldviews and past accomplishments. It promotes the dismissal of critical thinking, often through the employment of loaded language, such as the phrase, "environmental whacko" phrase of Rush

Limbaugh and his followers, "dittoheads" who do not understand science, even remotely, and would dismiss the threat of global warming, which threatens the existence of the human race, on the basis of their ignorance, where they are completely unwilling to learn.

It's possible that right-wing radio hosts like Rush Limbaugh and Michael Savage could be sponsored by clandestine branches of the Federal government. This should not come as completely surprising: the Church Committee found that the CIA had hired professors from "more than 100 universities" to promote government propaganda. The Committee reported that this approach was one of the CIA's most sensitive but also one of its most promising areas of endeavor, to be explained further in Four Arrows' forthcoming *The Language of Conquest: First Nations Scholars Talk Back* (2005). This work complements Carl Bernstein's earlier study, "The CIA and the Media", *Rolling Stone* (October 20, 1977), in which he reported the CIA had entered into secrecy agreements with some among our nation's most powerful media outlets, including CBS NEWS, TIME/LIFE, and *The New York Times*. With the backing of of giants of the industry, the domination of the news by the government ought to be expected. But the extent of that influence today has become truly appalling.

If it is folly to accept even well-reasoned conspiracy theories that rely upon logic and evidence in support of hypotheses (read this as "assassination science" when the hypothesis relates to a mysterious political death), then how are we to assess the established lies of corporate entities or governmental agencies? Were Watergate, the Pentagon Papers, the Contra fiasco, Iran scam, the MIA controversy, the rationale for the war in Iraq, innocent or inconsequential events? What has happened to America when black is white, up is down, and false is true? Have we lost our commitment to rationality, where we no longer hold beliefs on the basis of the available relevant evidence? Where we believe what is supported by the evidence when it meets appropriate standards? And where we hold our beliefs in suspense when the available evidence does not meet those standards?

The very idea that every theory that implies the existence of conspiracy ought to be rejected out of hand does not qualify as even remotely rational. Likewise, the very idea that every theory that implies the existence of conspiracy deserves to be accepted qualifies as equally irrational. The appropriate approach, needless to say, is that each case has to be evaluated on the basis of the evidence that is relevant and available in that case. It may be rational to reject the Flip Wilson hypothesis that, "The Devil made me do it.", because it is an untestable and thus unscientific explanation. But it does not appear rational to reject the existence of conspiracy in the death of JFK, David Kelly, or Paul Wellstone, for example, when there is ample, specific and detailed, evidence making those theories beyond reasonable doubt.

As even Chomsky acknowledges, it depends upon the strength of the evidence in each case. The authors are committed to the exercise of reason in the search for the truth about our recent history. We have found indication after indication, many of which are discussed in this book, of deceit and deception in the death of Paul Wellstone. A government that would send hundreds of thousands of young men and women into harm's way in a war that did not have to fought for reasons it could not explain and motives that were impure is not an administration that would hesitate to take out a single senator who stood in the way of its corrupt political agenda. Indeed, the occurrence of conspiracies, economic and political, appears to be a ubiquitous phenomenon of our time, where the assassination of Senator Paul Wellstone may be the latest but is surely not the last of that kind.

CHAPTER FIVE

THINKING THINGS THROUGH

"I'm not into conspiracy theories, except the ones that are true."
—Michael Moore

Scientific investigations of puzzling events, such as deaths that appear "fishy," are processes of successive approximation. Successive approximation demands that one account be succeeded by another as a consequence of the acceptance of new evidence, the rejection of old evidence, or the consideration of previously neglected alternative theories. These stages were exemplified in the study of the death of JFK, where initial accounts of three shots from a single shooter eventually gave way to more complex analyses on the basis of discoveries that the evidence had been altered, a cover-up had been imposed, and the alleged assassin, Lee Harvey Oswald, had been framed. Anyone who took for granted the authenticity of the evidence as presented in *The Warren Report* (1964), however, would have had good reasons to believe that the President had been killed by a "lone gunman". But those who want to perpetuate the government's account today can only do so by ignoring abundant new evidence.

FOUL BALLS AT THE NTSB

Other aircraft crashes have raised suspicions about the NTSB in the recent past. On January 31, 2000, Alaska Airlines Flight 261 crashed and killed Morris Thompson, his wife and daughter. Thompson was former Commissioner of Indian Affairs, and had been instrumental in the development of the Alaska Native Claims Settlement Act of 1971. ANCSA gave Alaskan Natives title to some of their ancestral lands, together with financial compensation for lands previously lost. Under Thompson's leadership, millions of dollars of annual revenues from native-owned regional corporations managed the lands and capital on behalf of the Native population. They opposed corporate oil interests. Thompson, shortly before the crash, had agreed to serve as chairman of the Alaska Federation of Natives' new "First Alaskans Foundation". Morris was a hero to Native Alaskans.

Thompson had prophetically stated that never before in American history had a group of Native Americans faced a more critical period than what lay ahead. The crash was a mystery. The NTSB blamed it on a "faulty stabilizer screw." The aircraft's mechanics didn't buy it.

According to John Quinn and Anthony Hilder, "Alaska Airlines Pilots, Crew Say NTSB 'Spin Story' is BS" (February 26, 2000):

> *Alaska Airlines personnel flatly rejected the National Transport Safety Board's "cover-up story." Employees were deeply disturbed by the fact that the airlines wouldn't furnish any info to their staff people. An inordinate amount of personnel had been absent the first three weeks after the crash due to "emotional trauma."*

> *"We're not buying the NTSB's Bull S..t" says one source. "The Feds have "tossed a foul ball & we are not hitting it" The, AK Airline's mechanics said that the "air holocaust" wasn't because of a faulty stabilizer screw, "That's so much hokum."*

This case strikes a chord with those skeptical of Wellstone's death. This case raises the same choice of explanations: accident or assassination? If we assume that the employees are justified in regarding the NTSB's account as hopelessly inadequate, then there would appear to be good reason to suspect that this "accident" might have been an assassination.

In a similar case, TWA Flight 800 exploded over Long Island on July 17, 1996 killing all 230 aboard. 258 eyewitnesses saw a streak of light rise like a missile and hit the flight. Sonar records show a high-speed craft high-tailing it out of that area of the ocean right afterwards. It's likely a military drill using missile defense technology had gone horribly awry.

However, NTSB chief James Hall, an old friend of Al Gore's from Tennessee, didn't call any of the eyewitnesses at the NTSB's hearings. Instead, the NTSB's own Dr. David Mayer took the stand and proclaimed that eye-witness testimony was of questionable value, since the memory is fallible. He mentioned that the FBI had failed to keep accurate notes or transcripts from their eyewitness interviews. Instead of levying criticism at the FBI, however, Mayer used this as another reason to discredit eyewitness testimony. When it came time to approve the proceedings, and James Hall's motion to approve needed a validation, he got an immediately second to his motion—from Carol Carmody.

THE EARLY ACCOUNTS

No doubt, because of his background with regard to scientific reasoning and critical thinking and more than 10 years devoted to the study of the death of JFK, Jim Fetzer was probably more sensitive to inconsistencies in the early accounts of the crash on October 25, 2002 than many of his fellow Minnesota residents. Some of his associates, including a few of his colleagues, however, shared his concerns. Through discussion with them and gathering evidence, he began to suspect something fishy was going on in relation to reports about the case and, subsequently, covering up what had actually taken place. His process of thinking things through as more and more evidence would became available offers a nice illustration of the process of successive approximation.

The basics of the death of Paul Wellstone appear to be the following: His plane was an Air King A100, one of the most reliable small planes in use today. It was piloted by two experienced fliers, with strong aviation credentials and training. The plane was approaching the Eveleth-Virginia Municipal Airport in overcast weather when it experienced a loss of control. It crashed and burned, killing all.

It will prove instructive to look at three key columns that Jim Fetzer published in *Reader Weekly*. The first of these, which was entitled, "What happened to Paul Wellstone?" (November 20, 2002, pp. 18-19), offers an example of the kinds of signs that struck Fetzer and some of his associates as rather odd, which made this—from their point of view—a puzzling event. By reflecting upon the full range of possible alternative explanations in this case, it became increasingly apparent to him and to others that something was going on here that exceeded what would be expected if the case had merely been an "accident".

What becomes most important about any specific event where conspiracy might be suspected is that it should be investigated thoroughly on its own terms. One of the most basic principles of scientific reasoning, for example, the requirement of total evidence, insists that, in the search for truth, all the evidence whose truth or falsity or presence or absence makes a difference must be taken into account.

An article in the *Duluth News Tribune* (October 30, 2002) states that, "Veteran pilots remain puzzled by the plane's bizarre path during the final moments of its flight Friday and theorize that a propeller failed or that the plane hit a flock of geese as it approached the airport. "Something dramatic happened and—whatever it was—it happened very quickly," said Bob Peasley, a longtime Northwest Airlines pilot, who has flown everything from two-seat Aeronca Champs to Boeing 757s."

The problem with these explanations is that communications between the pilots and the control tower were abruptly terminated as well when the plane went out of control. Not only could an Air King A100 fly on only one propeller, but the two pilots should have been able to notify the tower of their problem. There was nothing but silence.

Bill Wilkerson, who has been hiring pilots and leasing aircraft for more than 30 years, said, "This is not a plane that goes down in freezing rain. Visibility and conditions were not an issue in this accident. A pilot cannot fly this plane without an IFR (instrument flight rules) rating and hundreds of hours of experience. IFR rating means the plane can be landed completely on instrument with no visibility at all—fog, freezing rain, driving snow, etc. Wellstone's plane had two such pilots, which is unusual in itself." This makes it very difficult to imagine how the pilots or the plane could have been responsible for the crash that killed Paul Wellstone.

Wilkerson also was puzzled by the NTSB investigators, who have been emphatic that a severe fire had begun after impact: "In fact, that's about all they had to say, other than describing a crash perimeter that was preposterously small for serious investigation. There was mention of witnesses that saw the plane on fire on the way down, but they were neither identified nor repeated later in the day".

"Plain and simple", Wilkerson says, "based on my every experience with dedicated pilots and precision aircraft, planes like the A100 do not catch fire in spotty, wet weather and two experienced pilots are extremely unlikely to agree to fly under conditions they can't control. They were not suicide bombers. This plane was destroyed intentionally from afar".

One of Jim's colleagues, Tim Roufs, a professional anthropologist acustomed to making scientific observations, kept notes on national reports about the crash from Friday through Sunday. He was struck by the extent to which misleading and false information was being disseminated as though it were true. "They were clearly planting little thoughts in peoples' minds that simply were lies, like 'The plane crashed in freezing drizzle'", more than a half-day after it was clear that this was not the case.

"They also repeatedly, in national media, lied about the visibility, in spite of the fact that it was well documented by a UPS plane of slightly larger size flying into the airport just before that visibility wasn't that great, but that it was fine for professional pilots, that the airport manager who hopped in a plane when the Air King was overdue and flew to the wreckage, said the visibility was fine", where the FAA for the first few hours reported that the visibility had been fine but then—for reasons unknown—stopped reporting that.

Roufs also noticed that Denny Anderson, a retired private pilot himself, tried to explain that visibility had not been a factor and the difference between IFR and VFR (visual flight rules) to his audience. "It was almost mildly comical", Roufs said, "that Denny would review the difference between IFR and VFR flight rules after national news segments tried to obfuscate the difference, implying the pilots should have been flying VFR rules, which is ridiculous."

Roufs has extensive flight experience himself and has a son who is a professional pilot. "The plane was on straight final in, indicating no problems, going about 95 (or so knots), with all flaps set at 15 degrees (slight flaps down, but according to the Go Team all four working perfectly), 7 or so miles from touch down. Then, [according to the national media] 'for some mysterious reason that we may never know', the plane veered off course and took a steep dive."

The only alternative that fits the picture, in Roufs' view, is a suicide job by one of the pilots. "I would doubt that, but stranger things have happened." That two experienced pilots should have decided to commit suicide at the same time, of course, defies belief. It is difficult to imagine why, if one of them had tried to take the plane down, the other would not have communicated the information to the tower. Under these circumstances, regrettably, more sinister motives have to be taken seriously, including the possibility the crash resulted from a political conspiracy. In that case, his death would be an assassination.

Michael I. Niman, the professor cited above, raised the specter that this may indeed have been the case. "In a senate that is one heartbeat away from Republican control, Wellstone was more than just another Democrat. He was often the lone voice standing firm against the status-quo policies of both the Democrats and the Republicans. As such, he earned the special ire of the Bush administration and the Republican Party, who made Wellstone's defeat the party's number one priority this year." And it looked as though Wellstone's electoral defeat wasn't going to succeed.

The key to understanding the crash appears to be the complete cessation of communication between the pilots and the control tower. If the plane had lost a prop or hit a gaggle of geese, that could have been immediately reported to the tower. That did not happen. Something like a small bomb might have caused the crash; or perhaps an electromagnetic pulse, such as the police use to stop carjackers during high-speed chases; or an opiate-derivative gas of the kind the Russians used to overcome the Chechen rebels during the recent hostage crisis. It had to be something that caused a loss of communication as well as of control.

The latest reports from the *Star Tribune* (November 24, 2002) were not overly encouraging for those who would like to get to the bottom of this tragedy. The reporters on the story, Paul McEnroe and Tony Kennedy, are focusing on one of the pilot's lack of sleep the night before. This, of course, cannot explain why the co-pilot, who was also exceptionally well-qualified, would not have taken over, if the pilot had drifted off to sleep. Nor why the plane would have suddenly lost communication with the tower. But it does distract the American public.

That is a bad thing. Reports about the weather and visibility problems that appear to have made no difference to the crash should not be advanced as explanations. The same goes for the pilots. It is difficult to deny that by concealing the presence of two experienced pilots, the NTSB's spokesperson prevented the nation from learning right off the bat that pilot error was an extremely improbable occurrence. These are acts that mislead the nation.

THE COVER UP

Jim was not the only one who took exception to the original account of the crash, in spite of its widespread dissemination in the mass media. Bill Wilkerson, Michael Niman, and Tim Roufs were among others who were troubled by the lack of coherence between reports about the crash and their background knowledge, training and abilities based on their own experience. In another column entitled, "Paul Wellstone: More Questions, Fewer Answers" (January 9, 2003. pp. 12-13), Jim calculated the time it should have taken the FBI rapid response team to reach the scene of the crash. The results were striking.

The latest explanation, published in the *Star Tribune* (December 29, 2002), was that the pilots committed a blunder that turned into a stall, where airspeed had dropped to 85 knots. That theory does not withstand critical inspection, when the pilots' qualifications and the suitability of the weather are taken into account. Indeed, with this plane, a loud alarm sounds at 85 knots warning the pilot(s) that a stall is imminent, but leaving enough time to compensate. Experiments with these aircraft indicate that they only actually stall out below 70 knots.

This means other, less obvious, possible explanations have to be considered, even if, on moral, political, or personal grounds, we would prefer not to confront them. These include the possibility that the plane might have been disabled by a small bomb, by a canister of gas, or by an electromagnetic pulse. The most salient feature of the crash is the loss of communication that occurred simultaneously with the loss of control. This is difficult to explain by other, less sinister, causes. Neither pilot error, mechanical problems nor difficult weather can explain it.

It would have taken only a moment to report, for example, that the plane had come in out-of-alignment with the runway and that another attempt was being undertaken, as the stalling-out scenario would have it. "We're turning around and trying again." would have been enough to notify Gary Ulman, the Assistant Manager on duty at the Eveleth-Virginia airport, what was going on. Instead, Ulman heard the clicks of the microphone indicating that the runway lights were being activated—and nothing more. No words, no sounds—nothing but silence.

The plane had been expected to land on its flight from St. Paul between 10:20 and 10:30 AM as the Senator came to Eveleth for the funeral of a friend. Instead, a possible crash alert sounded at 10:50 and Ulman took to the air in an effort to locate the plane. Within a few minutes, he had located the crash site about two mile south of the airport, which was visible from blue smoke rising into the sky.

That in itself raises questions, because, as Christopher Bollyn of *The American Free Press* has observed, the fuselage burned for hours emitting blue smoke, when the aircraft's kerosene fuel, which was stored in tanks in its wings, should have emitted thick, black smoke instead. Why was the fuselage burning rather than the wings, especially when the wings were found separated from the fuselage? (http://www.thetruthseeker.co.uk/article.asp?ID=265).

The blue smoke allowed Ulman to locate the site of the crash between 10:55 and 11:00 AM. When he returned to the airport, he observed that local fire trucks had arrived. He took the fire chief up to survey the landscape and ascertain the most appropriate access route into the crash site, which was a road about 500 yards south of the wreckage. The time was 11:15 AM. Astonishingly, according to Rick Wahlberg, the Sheriff of St. Louis County, a team of FBI agents was on the crash site by noon.

Ulman told the *Reader* that, with all the phones he had to answer and people with whom he had to speak, he did not notice precisely when the FBI arrived, but he did notice their presence at the airport no later than 1 PM. As Christopher Bollyn discovered, these special agents were from the Twin Cities, not from Duluth, even though they had driven to Eveleth from Duluth using cars they had rented there. The FBI was certainly prompt to reach the crash site around noon, only about an hour after the occurrence of the crash had been confirmed by Ulman. And Gary had not even notified them.

This situation appears remarkable enough to undertake a reconstruction of what must have been the purported FBI time line, using MapQuest to estimate trips of this kind. The FBI Office in

Minneapolis is located at 111 Washington Avenue South, Minneapolis, MN 55401. Assuming that the plane the feds would use would be situated at Hubert Humphrey Terminal, which many special flights take as their point of departure, the distance turns out to be 12.41 miles, with a MapQuest estimated travel time of 17 minutes.

The HHT premise does not represent any stretch, moreover, since even if their plane had been located at one of the regional airports, such as Crystal or Eden Prairie, it would have taken at least 17 minutes to get there on the assumption that traffic is not very heavy. If the plane the feds were using had been flown earlier in the day, it might have been ready for departure almost upon their arrival. If it were the plane's first flight, however, preparation might have required 30 minutes, which could at least partially overlap with time spent reaching the airport.

If these guys did not have to pass through airport security, then they would not have lost additional time consumed by having their luggage examined, the contents of their pockets evacuated, and even their shoes removed. Still, it takes time to access and to board even their own private plane. Let us assume that the time from arrival at the airport to entering the plane was as few as 10 minutes. (That is a conservative estimate, all things considered, but let's acknowledge the efficiency of the federal government in times of crisis.)

Take off is not automatic, but might well consume anywhere from 10 to 30 minutes, especially if the plane they took was a regularly schedule commercial carrier. But let's make the simplifying assumption that the time from entering the plane to its actual departure from the airport could have been as little as 10 minutes. $17 + 10 + 10 = 37$ minutes at a minimum just to get the team to the plane and the plane in the air.

Jim has made the trip from the Twin Cities to Duluth International Airport many times, and a flight time of 40 minutes sounds about right to him. Assuming it was a small, private, "FBI ONLY" plane, then exiting the plane could be expedited. If it was an ordinary commercial flight with other passengers, however, then it might have taken longer. Let's assume the FBI charters its own and that it only took 5 minutes to exit. That means it had to have been $37 + 40 + 5 = 82$ minutes or 1:22 just to make it to the Hertz counter.

Here real problems can arise. Just how long do you think that it took the FBI to rent a car? Well, there are forms to fill out and licenses to produce and credit cards to process. If anyone has gone through this in less than 10 minutes, they probably deserve a prize. And then there's the matter of finding the car and packing the trunk.

Now traveling to Eveleth is something that Jim has done in the past—not to Eveleth, precisely, but to Gilbert. At a certain juncture in the road, Gilbert is to the right and Eveleth to the left. By MapQuest maps, the distance to Virginia, which is immediately adjacent to Eveleth, is 61 miles, with a driving time—absent a police escort—no less than 50 minutes. Even though he has a heavy foot, it has taken Jim and his wife that long to reach the junction.

These guys, of course, were not heading for a pleasant meal at The Whistling Bird, but for the gruesome wreckage of a King Air A100. Actually getting to the scene of the crash, of course, is something else entirely. According to the *Pioneer Press* (October 27, 2002), "Crews rode all-terrain vehicles to the site, about a half-mile from the nearest road, and had to vary their routes to avoid becoming mired in the swamp with up to 2 feet of water." Anybody's guess, but certainly it had to take another 10 minutes—at the absolute minimum—to arrive at the site.

So if we take 1:22 to get to Hertz, :10 more to rent and find the car, :50 to make it to Eveleth and another :10 to reach the actual site of the crash, then it should have taken these special agents at the very least 2:32 to make their trip, which remains a very conservative estimate. Yet according to the Sheriff of St. Louis County, they were on the scene at noon.

The crash, you may recall, did not actually occur until about 10:20 AM and had not been visually confirmed by Gary Ulman until 11 AM. Ulman did not notify the FBI that there had been a crash—ever. Even if a 911 operator had notified the FBI around 11 AM, how in the world did these very special agents know that they needed to head for the airport by 9:28 AM in order to be in Eveleth by noon? Perhaps the FBI possesses psychic powers and can anticipate the occurrence of tragedies of this kind in advance.

Or perhaps the FBI was in the position to anticipate the occurrence of this tragedy, without them? Even if we suppose the Sheriff of St. Louis County made a mistake in his recollection and that the FBI

AMERICAN ASSASSINATION

was only on the scene an hour later, as Ulman clearly recalls, that doesn't explain their arrival time. These agents might have had an additional hour but would still have had to depart for the airport by 10:28 AM.

The FBI might reply that the agents on the scene at noon had arrived from Bemidji rather than from Minneapolis or Duluth. But anyone familiar with a map of Minnesota will immediately perceive that this point of origin only makes the matter worse. It would have taken at least 1:40 minutes to reach Eveleth, which dictates a 10:20 time of departure. Conceivably, only agents from Duluth could have arrived by noon (with an 11:00 AM time of departure), but a female employee of the FBI office in Duluth assured Bollyn that Minneapolis agents had arrived first.

By securing the perimeter at the Wellstone crash site and discouraging photographs from being taken, the FBI was able to control access to the evidence. Experts have reported that planes of this kind are usually equipped with black boxes, because their clients are typically well-to-do, including celebrities and dignitaries. Indeed, the officials on the scene searched for a cockpit voice recorder for a day and a half before declaring there had not been one.

If indeed the FBI departed before the accident had even taken place, then the most reasonable explanation is that the FBI knew that it was going to occur. What other justification could possibly have warranted such a risky course of action, other than an deliberate cover up? The head of the NTSB, Carol Carmody, was even reported by the *Pioneer Press* (27 October 2002) to have explained, "She had consulted with the FBI and there was no intelligence information and no evidence in the wreckage to suggest any possibility of terrorism."

That's odd on several grounds. Surely it was the function of the NTSB to undertake the investigation of the causes of such a crash, including any possible indications of terrorism. The NTSB should be reporting to the FBI, not the other way around. Notably, Carmody is a former employee of the CIA. Furthermore, what are the indications of terrorism? A small bomb, perhaps, or a gas canister, or the use of EMP? How could these causes have possibly been ruled out at such an early stage?

As Christopher Bollyn astutely observes, if the wing section is charred but the tree is not, then either the wing was moved from the crash site (unlikely, and probably strictly forbidden in accident investigations) or the wing was on fire before the plane hit the ground (accounting for the lack of damage to the tree itself). This suggests that the small bomb hypothesis has to be taken seriously and that early reports from local residents, that there was an explosion, may have been actively suppressed.

Other reporters who have raised what should be easy questions about the FBI's arrival time include Michael Ruppert and Joe Taglieri. They have reported that Paul McCabe, a special agent from Minneapolis, has claimed the Minneapolis contingent only arrived about 3 PM. That contradicts Sheriff Wahlberg's report that he had arrived about 1:30 PM and saw Minneapolis FBI agents he knows personally who were already on the scene. When McCabe was asked about logs with official times, he became evasive, claiming, "We don't really keep log time, per se, like that," and suggested that times were not essential parts of investigative reports (http://mail-archive.com/ctrl@list-serv.aol.com/msg99496.html).

Ruppert contacted Lt. Tim Harkenen of the St. Louis Country Sheriff's Department, who maintained official logs of arrival times at the scene. After telling Ruppert that he would retrieve his files and check for the time, he ceased communication. The *Reader* left a message for Lt. Harkenen at his number at the Hibbing Sheriff's Office January 8, and we are still awaiting reply. Perhaps our new St. Louis' County Sheriff, Ross Litman, could contribute to clearing up this crucial point? It would be a good thing if our officials could help to answer questions rather than raise more of them.

Who could have directed the FBI to participate in such a cover-up, other than our own government? After all, Attorney General John Ashcroft eventually rose to power as a result of a similar accident. As Nafeez Ahmed, the author of *The War on Freedom* (2002), has observed, the Bush administration has justified blocking an inquiry into 9/11 on the ground that it would undermine its efforts to combat terrorism: "In other words, the administration (has) suppressed an inquiry into the greatest terror attack in U.S. history in the name of fighting terrorism."

ADDITIONAL NEW EVIDENCE

Jim's columns were attacked on various grounds, including that he had overlooked the obvious, namely: that something unexpected had happened. At least two of his critics published pieces criticizing him, including some who insisted that he should wait for the official NTSB report before offering his own assessment. But unless you already understood the relationship between the available relevant evidence and the alternative possible explanations, it would be impossible to evaluate whether or not the NTSB had done its job properly. A subsequent column, "What Happened, Once More, With Feeling" (*Reader Weekly* July 31, 2003) responded to those criticisms. The piece emphasized the crucial aspects of the available evidence that the NTSB overlooked or ignored, a practice first perfected by defenders of *The Warren Report* (1964). The points he made provide a nice example of the method of thinking things through.

A retired Air Force pilot, William Rees, took Jim to task for his columns exploring the death of Senator Paul Wellstone. In an earlier column, Rees explained that, in his opinion, "something unexpected happened", which, as Jim replied at the time, was hardly news. Here he emphasized the close margins within which pilots must operate, stating that a plane that might stall out at 80 knots may have a recommended final approach speed of 120 knots. What he says may be true in general, but appears to have scant relevance for the Wellstone crash. The NTSB's own simulation studies, which replicated the weather, the plane, and the pilots (by taking pilots from the same charter service) were unable to bring the plane down.

Rees stated that Jim's series should have ended with his first article, if not before. But that appears to be a difficult position to defend, especially given: the abrupt cessation of communication, the odd cell phone experience of John Ongaro, the FBI's extraordinarily rapid appearance on the scene, the exchange of roles between the FBI and the NTSB, the destruction of records of planes landing in Duluth that morning, the missing information from logs about those at the crash scene, the NTSB's cancellation of a public meeting for comments from citizens, previous attempts on Wellstone's life, the report of an insider that this had been a hit, and more. All of which Jim had been reporting.

It is Jim's opinion that the FBI probably arrived early in order to clean up evidence. Any watches or clocks at the scene might have contradicted the official findings. By predetermination, those findings were going to attribute the crash to pilot error, even though the NTSB's own simulations and the FAA's recent re-certification of pilot Richard Conry contradict it.

Jim has not covered all of these bases on his own but has benefited from the research of others, including members of http:/groups.yahoo.com/group/FETZERclaimsDEBUNK/, the forum that a former student, Thomas Bieter, created to assail his work. Considerable discussion has revolved about his use of the term "tower" and "communication", insofar as the Eveleth-Virginia does not have a physical tower. Jim explained that he was referring to the function, not the structure, but if there had been no genuine communication, it would have been impossible for there to have been "an abrupt cessation of communication" as his position implies. Since this became a hot topic on the forum, it would be a shortcoming of his research if he had this all wrong. A website forum member, Laura <twainable2@hotmail.com>, fortunately, has made several valuable discoveries, which she has posted on the forum that clarify this issue.

Ruppert and Taglieri, for example, quoted a piece from *The New York Times* (October 2002), where Carol Carmody cites "air traffic control records", that reported, "At 10:18, he was cleared for an east-west approach to the runway, and, according to radar, the plane was lined up with the runway. That was the last transmission conversation with the pilot, Ms. Carmody, a former CIA employee, said." Laura also discovered an NTSB Report (February 2003), which has 1519:12 (10:19) as the last "co-pilot/control tower communication". Both support the use of the word "communication", but the difference in time between 10:18 and 10:19 requires further consideration.

Another difference Laura noticed is that both NTSB reports have the 10:19 radar returns the same, at 3500 feet. But the November 2002 article (quoting *The Times*) has the last radar return 2 minutes later: "Two minutes later, radar recorded the last sighting of the plane at 1,800 feet and a speed of 85 knots just northeast of the accident site." The NTSB report (February 2003) says the last radar return was one minute later: "The last radar return was received at 1520:23. Radar data indicated N41BE was 4 miles southeast of EVM at an altitude of 2,300 feet with ground speed of 160 knots."

Laura provides links for comparison, which are available at the forum (the post which is being quoting here is message #535.) When another forum participant asked for more supporting information, Laura was able to oblige.In her message #544, she offered the following excerpts taken from an article published Monday, October 28, 2002, "Relatives visit Wellstone plane crash site", which is situated at http://www.brainerddispatch.com/stories/102802/sne_1028020018.shtml, namely:

> *EVELETH (AP)— A makeshift memorial adorned with roses and a picture of a smiling Paul Wellstone rests in a clearing about 100 feet from where a plane crashed killing the U.S. senator and seven others.*
>
> *"...Carol Carmody, acting chairwoman of the National Transportation Safety Board, said investigators reconstructed the flight based on information from radar, tapes and air traffic controllers.*
>
> *"At 10:01 A.M., controllers cleared the plane to approach the Eveleth airport. The pilot was then advised of light icing between 9,000 and 11,000 feet. At 10:10, the plane began its descent. Controllers cleared the pilot for an east-west approach to the airport at 10:18, the last exchange with the pilot."*

In addition, Laura provided a link to *The New York Times* article that she had cited, which may be found at http://www.nytimes.com/2002/10/28/politics/28CRAS.html. And in her message #545, she posted excerpts from the *St. Paul Pioneer Press*, which may be found at http://www.geocities.com/wellstonecrash/drifting.html.

"Two Minutes Before Crash, Plane Was Already Drifting", by Hannah Allam, Todd Nelson, Phillip Pina, and Charles Laszewski, *The Pioneer Press* (Monday, 28 October 2002):

> *...The flight, which left the Twin Cities at 9:37 A.M. Friday, had been routine until its final minutes, according to a reconstruction of the flight based on radar data reviewed by investigators from the National Transportation Safety Board.*

At 10:18 A.M., the pilot got clearance to land at the Eveleth Virginia Municipal Airport, lined the aircraft up with the runway and was heading straight west. Everything appeared routine, said Carol Carmody, acting NTSB chairwoman.

There was no evidence on the controller's part or from the pilot's voice that there was any difficulty," Carmody said of the last conversation between the pilot and the ground. No reported problems. No expressed concern.

Something changed in the next 60 seconds, because at 10:19 A.M. the twin-engine aircraft began drifting slightly to the south, radar showed. The last appearance on radar came about two minutes later, as the plane was just north of the crash site's east side.

His critics have been adamant that John Ongaro has "backed off" and now thinks his odd cell phone experience was nothing out of the ordinary. In the front-page story on Thomas Bieter's threatened lawsuit that appeared in the *Minneapolis Star-Tribune* (June 3, 2003), for example, John played down its significance.

John had been even quoted as saying, "It's not unusual for cell phones to cut out, especially in northern Minnesota." That was most certainly not his response at the time, when he initially contacted Jim after Jim had published his first two columns on this subject and made a few appearances on radio talk shows. As we showed earlier, Mr. Ongaro said the opposite in his email.

To revisit this email, let's recall that Mr. Ongaro wrote, "Knowing Congressman Oberstar quite well, I decided to forward my email onto his Duluth office. Ironically, they emailed me back with a message that stated that the FBI had already informed them that they had already investigated any possibility of foul play and had ruled it out."

This experience with Congressman Oberstar, whom Mr. Ongaro knew personally, is extraordinarily disconcerting. This is very much like the announcements from Dallas that three shots had been fired by a lone gunman within a few minutes of the event. Some reports are simply incredible on their face. So John Ongaro was not minimizing the importance of his experience at the time.

Indeed, more than two months later, it was still very much on his mind. He sent Jim the following post on March 16, 2003. Ask yourself if this post comes from a man who does not believe something suspicious occurred in the death of Paul Wellstone? He makes a very simple but powerful suggestion based upon statistical considerations, which most Americans would never pause to consider. Admire, as we do, the clarity of his reasoning about this event and the context of its occurrence:

Date: Sun, 16 Mar 2003 00:39:09 -0500 (EST)
From: ‹email address omitted›
Subject: john ongaro has sent you an article from NPR Online
To: jfetzer@d.umn.edu

This NPR article was sent to you by john ongaro (email address omitted) with the following message:

This segment on EMP ran on "talk of the nation," yesterday. I thought you would find it interesting...By the way, couldn't one of your colleagues in statistics rate what the odds were of two Democrat U.S. Senators getting killed in plane crashes in the final 10 days of a neck and neck election within 2 years of each other, then having Ashcroft directly and indirectly involved, the same former CIA, NTSB investigator, etc, etc? I bet one might have a better chance of winning the lottery, twice. Once people saw what the odds of this all happening were, maybe then this would be construed as perhaps more than the "mother of all coincidences." Call me, I might have another lead for you.

The article title is "NPR : News Roundup: EMP Bomb" and can be found at: http://discover.npr.org/rundowns/segment.jhtml?wfld=1192402

Portions of John's original post were published previously in the *Reader,* but the totality of his message, and his subsequent correspondence—have become of immense importance to understanding the case. Jim has not been surprised that he has "backed off" recently as this matter has received more and more attention from the press and the public. John makes his living as a lobbyist for the City of Duluth, where he deals with members of both parties in the state legislature. Jim suspects that he has wanted to move off the hot seat on this one, because it is not a popular issue, especially withRepublicans.

Indeed, we can sympathize, because the verbal assaults to which Jim have been subjected on Bieter's forum. They have far exceeded the boundaries of civilized discourse and on occasion implied bodily harm. So, we can understand Ongaro's current attitude. But we have meanwhile discovered a web site featuring the kind of sound that would be made by one type of EMP weaponry, which sounds very much like what John Ongaro described, which may currently be found on *www.assassinationscience.com* under the heading, "HERF Data #1."

ELECTROMAGNETIC WEAPONS

Since John Ongaro wondered whether his odd cell phone experience might have been related to the use of a directed energy weapon, it would be appropriate to provide some background about weapons of this kind.

There are whole families of new Radio Frequency (RF) and ElectroMagnetic Pulse (EMP) weaponry, including High-Energy Radio Frequency (HERF) guns, some of which have been around at least since the mid 1990s. But even Rees appears to be ignorant of these advances in technology. "I may be out of date," he wrote, "but last I knew a nuclear detonation is required to produce an Electromagnetic Pulse. I am unaware that such a force has been harnessed in an anti-aircraft weapon, especially one small enough for assassins to skulk around in swampy woods."

Actually, Rees is *quite* out of date. EMP pulses are by-products of nuclear explosions, which first led to their discovery. A google search turns up hundreds of sources with more current information. One of Jim's collaborators on Zapruder film research, John P. Costella, earned his Ph.D. in physics specializing in electromagnetic theory. Jim asked Dr. Costella to explain the general features of the use of devices of this kind in language that a layman can understand. Here's what he had to say:

> The world around us is surrounded by electromagnetic waves. Some of us may recall building crystal radio sets when we were young. Even then, radio waves were strong enough to power the earpiece without the need for a separate power source. Radar tracks aircraft and weather by sending out beams of radio waves and measuring how much is bounced back. Cell phones communicate with cable phone networks by means of high frequency radio waves and internet carriers communicate

with satellites using powerful microwave transmitters, where radiowaves and microwaves are different types of electromagnetic waves.

All electronic devices can be disrupted if subjected to strong enough electromagnetic waves. Your home music system may click or pop when a lamp is switched on. Your TV may go fuzzy when someone plugs in a power drill. Electromagnetic interference is a troublesome fact of life. And there is an entire federal agency dedicated to making sure that all of our modern electronic devices can function in the same house or work place. Interference can be reduced by "shielding" a device in a metallic cage, but the more metal a manufacturer uses, the more costly and weighty the device becomes.

Today, aircraft systems are dominated by electronics. The amount of "shielding" possible is limited by the need to keep the aircraft light enough to fly. The most disastrous times for electromagnetic interference to the control system is during takeoff and landing, when there is little room for error nor time to correct it. This is why you are told not to use cell phones, computers, or any other electronic device when an aircraft is taking off or landing.

But if a cell phone or a Gameboy could cause an aircraft to crash, what about all the other electromagnetic waves flying about our modern world? Both NASA and the FAA have performed detailed research on this question in recent years. One NASA report is at www-sdb.larc.nasa.gov/Air_Support/aries/papers/electromagnetic.pdf, providing a chilling history of crashes caused by inadvertent electromagnetic waves.

In the 1980s, for example, five different Black Hawk helicopters dove into the ground and crashed when they flew near radio transmitters. It was found that the rear stabilization control system was vulnerable to electromagnetic interference. In the early 1990s, six F-111 fighters crashed or aborted their missions, due simply to the radio transmissions of other U.S. aircraft involved in the same missions. Around the same time, the NTSB concluded that seven Piper Malibu broke up in mid-flight because of electromagnetic interference to the auto pilot, which had been reported by 300 other pilots of similar aircraft.

A 1983 crash of a Tornado fighter was later found to be due to the electromagnetic interference of a "Voice of America" transmitter with its air data computer. In the early 1990s, four different airline carriers reported widespread interference with avionics systems in flight over the Caribbean. These were traced to high-power electromagnetic surveillance carried out by the U.S. military—both shipboard and airborne—to track drug traffic in the region. It has even proposed that the crash of TWA 800 in 1996 might have been due to electromagnetic interference.

The FAA has also investigated in detail the risks of electromagnetic fields. A 1999 report is http://aar400.tc.faa.gov/acc/accompdocs/99-50.pdf. They investigated in detail 893 "emitters" of electromagnetic waves—radio and television transmitters, radar and satellite uplink transmitters, and large microwave communication systems— around just the cities of Denver, CO, and Seattle, WA. They report that there are some 50,000 similar major "emitters" of electromagnetic waves in the U.S. and Western Europe.

The FAA estimated the probability that a single flight into or out of one of these cities would crash due to electromagnetic interference. This involved estimating probabilities that the flight path would come too close to an emitter, that an emitter would transmit on just the right frequency and in the direction of the aircraft, and that the interference would cause a catastrophic crash. The main conclusions of the report address proposed new shielding levels for aircraft, which are or appear to be appropriately safe, where the average number of flights expected between catastrophic failures due to this cause would be between 100,000 and 500,000.

Buried here, however, are corresponding estimates for aircraft already manufactured under less stringent guidelines. Reconstructing the figures from those contained in the report, a flight in an aircraft manufactured after the release of the 1989 standard would incur a catastrophe roughly ever 5,000 flights. For an aircraft manufactured according to 1984 standards, the figure drops precipitously to a catastrophe expected for every 33 flights. These figures, of course, reflect approximately how often the wrong conditions might be expected to be encountered by aircraft merely by chance.

These estimates may be conservative and there are many factors involved in determining whether this has practical implications for any aircraft now flying. However, it does high-light that completely accidental electromagnetic interference has become a major safety concern in the modern world of burgeoning electromagnetic communications. So if that is the score regarding aircraft crashes merely by chance, then just how difficult would it be to bring down an aircraft using an electromagnetic emitter on purpose?

This obviously depends on the resources available and the age and type of aircraft under consideration. Flight paths are already designed to avoid known electromagnetic emitters by some safe margin. If one were simply to gain control of one of these emitters, aim it directly at an aircraft, and transmit with sufficient power at the right frequencies, the probability of catastrophic failure would skyrocket. If we move into the realm of special purpose EM-weaponry—obviously possessed in copious quantities by the military and anyone else with similar desires—then literally the sky is the limit.

Some may be uneasy to learn that today's aircraft—par-ticularly, aging aircraft—should be so vulnerable to relatively simple and inexpensive attack. The explanation is that, most of the time—even almost all of the time—no one is actively try-ing to cause an aircraft to crash. Regulatory frameworks and agencies like the FAA attempt to ensure that such catastrophes do not occur very frequently by chance. Any "cowboys" shoot-ing electromagnetic waves into the air at random, moreover, would quickly be detected by the U.S. military, either through ground-based detection or through satellite surveillance.

It would only be in the case of very carefully planned or specifically targeted use of EM-weaponry that the culprits could escape detection by the U.S. military. Unless, of course, the cul-prits were the U.S. military itself. As 9/11 has taught us, the practicalities of economic life dictate that safety measures are very finely balanced against commercial costs and corporate profits. Anyone who could not conceive of an aircraft being brought down by even a relatively small-sized EM emitter, therefore, ought to pause the next time they continue to use their laptop computers or cell phones when their planes are about to take off. It might turn out to be their final flight.

Costella's observations make it all too apparent that weapons of this kind not only exist, but that the threats they pose to aircraft are very real. These threats affect every passenger, every flight. This means that even though most Americans are unaware of the potential of these weapons—with former Air Force pilot Rees being a prime example—it would be a blunder to not consider the possibility that EMP weapons could have been employed in the Wellstone crash. Before we continue our exploration of this technology and why we believe it is likely that they may have been used to assassinate the Senator, we will first analyze the official government account.

CHAPTER SIX

THE OFFICIAL STORY

The only time you should vote is when you really feel like you have all of the information.

—Paul David Wellstone

On November 18, 2003, five people from the National Transportation and Safety Board participated in a telephone conference to vote on the "findings" presented to them by Charlie Pereira, the Aircraft Performance Group Chairman for the Wellstone crash investigation. Pereira, holder of a 1989 B.S. degree in Aeronautical Engineering from Embry-Riddle Aeronautical University, concluded that the pilots came in too slow on approach and that had apparently caused the plane to stall and crash. The NTSB officially and unanimously adopted the conclusion that this pilot error was to blame for the death of Senator Paul Wellstone, his wife, daughter, staff and crew.

The 76-page NTSB report is lacking in many respects, not only for what it says, but for what it does not say. Here we quote the most significant statements in this text and offer reflections that challenge both its thoroughness and its assumptions:

> Loss of Control and Impact with Terrain Aviation Charter, Inc. Raytheon (Beechcraft) King Air A100, N41BE Eveleth, Minnesota October 25, 2002

> Aircraft Accident Report NTSB/AAR-03/03 PB 2003-910403 Notation 7602

> National Transportation Safety Board Washington, D.C.

The report begins with an "Executive Summary" in which the NTSB lists a number of "facts" without comment. These facts paint a decidedly predetermined picture that completely ignores any possibility of an assassination:

The plane crashed while the flight crew was attempting to execute the VOR approach to runway 27.

According to expert testimony, there is no substantial reason to conclude that the pilots would have had any trouble executing the approach based on VOR operation, given weather, radio communication, visual sightings, pilot training and experience:

The crash site was located about 1.8 nautical miles southeast of the approach end of runway 27.

This location and the position of the aircraft show the airplane on a path opposite that of a runway approach. That means this plane did not crash while in line with an approach but rather it crashed after having turned in the opposite direction. A turn like this makes little sense if the crash was simply an error on approach.

The airplane was destroyed by impact forces and a post-crash fire.

In fact, only the fuselage was destroyed by fire. The wings and tail section were not. A number of experts testified about the unusual nature of the fire that consumed the aircraft. Mechanics who have specialized in working on the King Air have stated that it would be improbable for the fuselage to burn if the wings had been separated from the fuselage, as occurred here as a result of hitting trees before crashing to the earth, because all the fuel is stored in the wings. Interestingly, the least burned item in this crash was one of the wing surfaces. The configuration of damage to the plane was odd.

Also a number of individuals stated that the smoke was blue, consistent with an electrical fire, not a fuel fire. How would an electrical fire have started? Why would there have been no coarse black smoke, since that would be normal for the type of fuel the plane had in its wing tanks? What about witnesses interviewed by the NTSB who thought they might have seen a flash of fire while the plane was still in the sky?

The NTSB determines that the probable cause of this accident was the flight crew's failure to maintain adequate airspeed, which led to an aerodynamic stall from which they did not recover.

This is the most important sentence in its entire report, implying that the pilots lost track of their altitude and airspeed. The NTSB will say more on this later, as will we.

After this opening summary, a list of findings follows, the most important of which we offer here.

> At 0716, the pilot called the Princeton Automated Flight Service Station for an abbreviated weather briefing. The AFSS specialist informed the pilot that cloud conditions at EVM were reported as scattered at 1,000 feet and overcast at 2,000 feet and that visibility was reported as 4 statute miles in light snow. (Unless otherwise indicated, all altitudes in this report are reported as height above mean sea level (msl.) Altitudes referenced from surface weather observations and forecasts (TAF) are reported as height above ground (agl).) At about 0719, the pilot stated, "You know what, I don't think I'm going to take this flight." At 0817, the pilot contacted AFSS and asked, "Can you give me Eveleth weather right now?" The AFSS specialist stated that the latest automated weather for EVM was issued at 0754 and that it indicated calm winds, visibility of 3 statute miles in light snow, and an overcast cloud ceiling at 900 feet. At 0818, the pilot began filing an IFR flight plan with an estimated departure from STP of 0920. At 0840, the pilot called Aviation Charter's director of charter and indicated that he was getting conflicting guidance from the Senator's staff and he did not feel comfortable deciding whether or not to make the flight. The director stated that the pilot did not seem overly stressed, just concerned about doing a good job.

In this section the NTSB report has combined facts that demonstrate that weather was not a significant issue, while at the same time suggesting that something was bothering the pilot. Is this evidence that the pilots felt that they did not have the skills to fly in this weather? Recall that other witnesses said they felt the pilot's voice sounded somewhat distant or strange. Is there any particular significance to these reports? Should they have been mentioned in the NTSB report?

By 1017:35, the airplane had leveled off at 3,500 feet with the airspeed decreasing through about 190 KCAS. At 1018, when the airplane was less than about 1/2 mile south of the published VOR runway 27 approach course, the DLH approach control south radar controller advised, "one zero miles from the vor turn left heading three zero zero maintain three thousand five hundred til established on the final approach course cleared for the vor runway two seven approach Eveleth." The copilot acknowledged the instruction at 1018. Radar data indicate that shortly thereafter, the airplane began turning left while maintaining 2,500 feet and slowing through about 164 KCAS. Almost immediately after the airplane began its left turn, it overshot the approach course and traveled for almost 1 mile north of the course until establishing a ground track of about 262 degrees.

The NTSB is saying that the plane "overshot" the approach course while still about 10 miles out. Is this proof of pilot incompetence? According to a number of staff at Eveleth Airport and according to one witness who lives nearby, such an "overshoot" was not at all unusual. Many pilots when turning left do so very shortly after the controller's instructions. One mile comes up fairly rapidly at this speed and it is relatively easy to make up for going past the exact course angle called out by the controller. John Kaukola was one of the witnesses the NTSB interviewed. He has watched planes from his backyard land at Eveleth for ten years. He said the plane had been initially lined up well upon approach after corrections had been made.

At 1019:12 the controller stated, "king air one bravo echo change to advisory frequency approved; advise cancellation of ifr with Princeton flight serve when on ground" and the co-pilot acknowledged the instruction at 1019:20, saying "roger that we'll contact Princeton on the ground four one bravo echo good day." This was the last transmission received from the accident airplane. At this time radar data indicate that at this time the airplane began its descent from 3,500 feet and that its airspeed stopped decreasing at about 155 KCAS and began increasing.

Close to the time the plane started heading off course and diving toward the ground, the pilots were obviously unconcerned. One of them even reportedly said, "Have a good day." According to a number of NTSB reports, accidents usually result from a successive series of mistakes that eventually add up to the fatal one, but at this late stage there do not appear to be any mistakes that have happened.

Nonetheless, pilot error was the focus of attention from the beginning of the investigation, a focus that is generally not given such emphasis so early in an investigation when there are no good reasons to suspect it. A conclusion is being promoted before the evidence has been evaluated. In this context, even the use of the phrase "accident airplane" is a loaded phrase that assumes the crash was an accidental occurrence.

> The airplane's airspeed increased to about 170 KCAS and its vertical speed increased through 1,000 feet per minute as it descended through 3,200 feet. The vertical speed peaked at about 1,400 fpm. At 1020, as the airplane passed through south of the approach course about 5 miles east of the runway 27 threshold, a slight right turn was initiated and the airplane's airspeed and vertical speed began decreasing. The airplane established a ground rack of about 269 degrees. The last two radar returns indicate that the airplane had slowed to about 76 KCAS at 1,800 feet.

Since the radar returns are widely known to be "inconsistent" under 2500 feet, how can anyone be sure that this was the speed? This is significant since the cause of the crash, a stall, which the NTSB will allege had occurred, relates to too low airspeed.

> One witness indicated that he saw the airplane to the west of his location approximately 4.5 miles east of the runway 27 threshold "just beneath a low layer of clouds." He stated that he noticed the landing gear was down. (Visibility of 1 statute mile was required to execute the VOR runway 27 approach.)

There were numerous witnesses who testified before the NTSB with decidedly more significant narrative than this, yet their testimony is not mentioned. Furthermore, the NTSB conducts hearings that are public in about 50% of its investigations, especially those considered "high profile." Yet there was no public hearing in this investigation that would have allowed eyewitness testimony. John Kaukola, who was one of the testifying witnesses, stated that as he was listening to the plane and tracking it by the sound of the engines, "All of the sudden, well before the plane should have been at the airport," the sound of the engines was gone. "The sound really went down; not like they shut it off, not like the engines quit. He just eased back on the throttle and I thought, 'Boy, he powered back soon,' and I turned my back away and then I heard the boom."

Closer to the crash site—about a mile away—Megen Williams tells a similar story. She was resting that Friday morning with her bedroom window only partially open when she heard the plane. Like Kaukola, an abrupt drop in engine noise right before the crash caught Williams' attention. Yet the NTSB report says nothing about their reports, even though they provide corroborating testimonies.

> The Operations Group listened to the recorded ATC voice communications to identify which flight crew member was operating the radios for each transmission. Although the group determined that the copilot made all but one of the transmissions to ATC, it could not determine who was the flying pilot, that is, the pilot manipulating the airplane's flight controls, during the flight.

Ultimately, NTSB concludes that Richard Conry, the pilot, was probably at the controls, but to make the case for their conclusion, we must believe that both the pilot and the co-pilot were incompetent at the controls of this airplane. And Conry had passed his FAA "flight check" only two days before the fatal crash. Which means that, as far as the FAA was concerned, Conry was fully competent to be in command of that aircraft.

> The airplane impacted the ground at an elevation of 1,364 feet ...about 1/4 mile south-southwest of the last radar return, 1.8 miles southeast of the approach end of runway 27.

Recall that elevations can be reported as above sea level or above the ground. This obviously refers to a sea level measurement. Again, there is no clarification in the report that the plane was facing the opposite direction of the runway.

PILOT ERROR

The conclusion of the NTSB was that pilot error caused the crash. The local mainstream press and the Wellstone family also agreed with this, at least in public. In the case of the family, they had to, in order to successfully sue the charter company. But let's look closely at what the NTSB said about pilot competence. We'll list the NTSB findings and add commentary. Then, at the end of the section about the pilots, we'll question the "facts" used to conclude that the pilots were incompetent and made fatal mistakes.

> The pilot (Richard Conry) worked at Simmons Airlines, doing business as American Eagle, from November 1989 until April 27, 1990. Simmons could not provide investigators with any documentation regarding his employment at the company. The Safety Board's investigation was unable to determine if the pilot gained any additional flying experience while employed at Simmons. (Simons did not have the pilot's employment records because he had last been employed at the company more than 5 years previously.)...

> From Feb 2-20, 1990, the pilot stood trial on criminal charges for mail and wire fraud. He was convicted and sentenced to 2 years in prison and 5 years probation. The pilot submitted a letter of resignation to Simmons dated April 27, 1990. He was released from prison on November 8, 1991 and served probation which he completed on November 7, 1996.

The FAA does not restrict a pilot from flying because of felony records that do not relate to drug use. A mail or wire fraud felony also would not in itself demonstrate incompetence to fly an airplane. Some might ask, Why would Aviation Charter, for example, hire a felon? Would someone with financial challenges as Conry had (both he and his co-pilot, Guess, worked extra jobs) and a criminal record be likely to be complicit in an unethical scheme of some sort? These factors could be elements of a very different kind of theory about the crash.

The criminal history, and the financial desperation of both pilots is brought up by the NTSB, but for the wrong reasons. The NTSB seems to be implying that the record of the pilots implies pilot incompetence. But we are not interested in character assassination. We propose that the criminal past of the pilots logically leads us to consider that the pilots could have been manipulated into unwittingly participating in the crash.

Perhaps they were convinced to carry something on board. Perhaps someone paid them to carry this thing on, telling them it was contraband or narcotics, when really it was a tracking device, or a bomb. This would explain why, after the accident, one of the weather briefers told the NTSB that Conry had sounded stressed and apprehensive about the flight. The briefer, recall, was concerned someone was pressuring Conry to make the flight.

We do not know for certain this was the case, but the theory becomes more appealing when we confront the "coincidence" that the co-pilot had ties to alleged 9/11 criminal, Zacharias Moussaoui (discussed below). We are implying that these questions point to possibilities that are at least as meaningful as the single-minded assumption that there should be some correlation between a criminal record for a racketeering charge and the ability to fly an airplane. Surely these properties are ordinarily independent.

> According to Aviation Charter records, the pilot had flown 5,116 total flight hours, 598 of which he flew with the company, 200 hours of which were as pilot-in-command in King Airs. A search of FAA and company records showed no accident or incident history or enforcement or disciplinary actions, and a search of the National Driver Register database found no record of driver's license revocation or suspension.

This NTSB finding does not seem to support the incompetent pilot error assumption. Also, according to the NTSB's own sources, several Aviation Charter pilots who had flown with the "accident" pilot described him as "very meticulous," "by the book," "calm," and "laid back," "diligent in his use of checklists," and "could be assertive, if necessary." Even more positive assessments were not included in the report.

> Another company King Air copilot indicated that during a flight with the accident pilot about 2 months before the accident, the pilot did not have his navigational radio tuned to the VOR in use for the approach, which caused the pilot's course deviation indicator (CDI) to provide erroneous indications during the entire approach. The copilot was the flying pilot and had his navigation radio tuned to the correct VOR and completed the approach without incident.

This is the first of several reports suggesting that Conry was incompetent as a pilot. Yet no reports about negative behaviors of the "accident" pilot were ever reported to company management. It is likely that a thorough investigation of any pilot with the intent to find fault would find histories of relatively minor incidents such as this. In this case, since the copilot was the flying pilot, Conry's mistake was not important enough to report to management.

Pilot and copilot relationship seems to be a factor of some confusion in the NTSB report. The report implies later that he let his copilots fly because of his own incompetence. Yet, most copilots were appreciative about Conry's doing this and did not draw such a conclusion. Also, Conry and Guess, who served as copilot of the aircraft, had flown four flights together before the "accident" flight, all of which were in King Airs. The wives of both pilots reported neither ever mentioned having any problems flying with one another.

> The pilot's logbook indicated that he had flown Senator Wellstone at least 12 times.

When Four Arrows interviewed Jeff Blodgett (April 7, 2004), Wellstone's campaign manager and the Director of Wellstone Action, a program founded by the Senator's sons with money won from the lawsuit to continue Wellstone's important agendas, Blodgett was personally convinced that the pilots were incompetent and that the charter company had committed fraud for having hired them. He himself had also flown with the pilots and Wellstone. It was difficult for Four Arrows to suppress his puzzlement why evidence for their incompetence had not emerged before the crash.

> Safety Board investigators reviewed the pilots' logbooks and discovered a variety of disparities such as different departure and arrival airports for the same flights, different flight times, different total flight hours during certain periods, etc.

Is the fact that two different pilots who fill out logbooks separately and sometimes hours after the flight have disparities appropriate evidence of pilot incompetence?

> As part of his employment, the copilot observed two complete sequences of systems training lessons and one complete sequence of flight-training lessons. He also received seven flight-training lessons in an A320 simulator. The copilot's instructor during these lessons twice noted that the copilot

needed to be reminded to keep his hands on the throttles during approaches. Northwest records indicate that the copilot was not able to successfully complete this stage of the training program. According to his supervisor, the copilot's ability to learn and retain the details of the A320 systems was far lower than that of fellow trainees with comparable flying experience. He added that, by the time the other trainees finished learning to teach all of the A320 systems lessons, the copilot had mastered less than half of the lessons.

Since the NTSB concluded that Conry was flying the plane, not copilot Guess, this evidence of the copilot's incompetence may or may not be relevant. In any event, according to Aviation Charter records, the copilot had flown about 701 total flight hours, 304 hours of which were with the company, 107 hours of which were in King Airs. He had flown approximately 69, 54, and 36 hours in the last 90, 60, and 30 days, respectively, before the accident. His last recurrent ground training occurred on August 2, 2002. His last proficiency check occurred on August 3 and 4, 2002, and records from the check indicated that the check was satisfactorily completed. A search of FAA and company records showed no accident or incident history or enforcement or disciplinary actions, and a search of the National Driver Register found no record of driver's license having been subject to revocation or suspension.

The copilot's performance was acceptable at the conclusion of ground training. Pilots who had flown with the copilot described him as friendly, happy, organized, motivated, and eager to learn. Several pilots who had flown with the copilot described him as not assertive and expressed concern about his flying skills, especially his inability to land the airplane without assistance.

In addition, the pilot reportedly had a reputation for allowing his copilots to perform most of the flying, which might have reduced his flight proficiency and skills. Postaccident statements from Aviation Charter pilots and other personnel indicate that both pilots often exhibited potentially serious performance deficiencies during flight operations. Therefore, the Safety Board concludes that both pilots had previously demonstrated potentially serious performance deficiencies during flight operations consistent with below-average flight proficiency.

This last quote sums up the case of the NTSB and presumably of the attorneys who sued Aviation Charter on behalf of the surviving Wellstone family members. Before analyzing the source of the NTSB conclusions about pilot and copilot incompetence, let's look at an independent news journalist's conclusions as they were reported on Saturday, October 26, 2002, in the *St. Paul Pioneer Press* offering a contrary view. Note especially the phrases we have emphasized, especially the reference to the fact that Conry was Senator Wellstone's favorite charter captain, a matter confirmed by the NTSB itself: "According to the Senator's campaign scheduler, Conry and another pilot were the Senator's favorite Aviation Charter captains. The Senator trusted them and his staff requested Conry or the other captain when scheduling the Senator's trips" (NTSB Factual Report, February 20, 2003, p. 8). After having more than twelve trips with the pilot, if he was incompetent, then one would be inclined to suppose that the Senator or the members of his staff would have noticed long before the crash.

In the same article, "Charter, 2 Families Mourning Flight," Hannah Allam states:

> One pilot was a veteran airman requested by clients for his reliability and experience. The other was a recently engaged young man who loved to fly and collected model planes. Capt. Richard Conry, 55, and co-pilot Michael Guess, 30, were among the eight people killed when the twin-engine private plane carrying Sen. Paul Wellstone crashed Friday near Eveleth, Minn. The men often flew with the senator, co-workers said, and were experienced pilots. Far away from teary-eyed politicians and TV cameras, workers at Eden Prairie-based Executive Aviation privately mourned their colleagues during what a spokeswoman described as a "somber and silent" day.

Earlier we said that attempting to relate the pilot's racketeering conviction to being knowingly or unknowingly part of an assassination conspiracy is approximately equally plausible as the NTSB's relating it to the pilot's flying skills. In this case, the idea gains credibility when we consider the copilot's encounter with and possible acquaintance of Zacarias Moussaoui, who was tried on several counts of murder for participating in the 9/11 attack on the Twin Towers.

Moussaoui's story is striking. He was first arrested in Minnesota on August 16, after officials of a flight school, the Pan Am International Flight Academy, in Eagan, MN, a suburb of Minneapolis, tipped off the FBI that he was seeking flight training on a Boeing 747 jumbo jet. His conduct aroused suspicion. He was evasive about his personal background. He paid the $6,300 fee for the training in cash. He insisted on training to fly a jumbo jet despite an obvious lack of skill even with small planes. He did not want to learn how to take off or land, only how to handle the jet in the air. Moussaoui's instructor and a vice president of the flight school would later brief two Democratic congressmen from the Minneapolis area about their repeated efforts to get the FBI to take an interest in Moussaoui's conduct.

One of these congressmen was James Oberstar, who would later assure John Ongaro that the FBI had ruled out any foul play in the Wellstone crash. The unnamed instructor and school official told Oberstar that it took four to six phone calls to the FBI to find an agent who would help. The instructor became so frustrated by the lack of response that he said to the FBI, "Do you realize that a 747 loaded with fuel can be used as a bomb?" (These accounts first appeared in the *Minneapolis Star-Tribune*, then in *The New York Times* on December 22, 2001. See http://www.webcom.com/hrin/magazine/pilot.html)

Moussaoui was detained by the Immigration and Naturalization Service on charges of violating the terms of his visa. Local FBI investigators in Minneapolis immediately viewed Moussaoui as a terrorist suspect and sought authorization for a special counter-intelligence surveillance warrant to search the hard drive of his home computer. This was rejected by higher-level officials in Washington, who claimed there was insufficient evidence to meet the legal requirements for the warrant. (See Patrick Martin, wsws.org, January 5, 2002.) Moussaoui watched the events of 9/11 from his jail cell. As of this writing, his case remains interesting for a number of reasons, including his claim that the FBI and even his lawyers were trying to kill him, which resulted in a judge allowing him to defend himself. A complex series of legal issues and his lengthy appeal have yet to be resolved. What may matter more is that Copilot Guess went to school at University of North Dakota, where he earned a degree in aeronautics.

The coincidences start getting really intriguing when we also consider this story: Moussaoui applied for a short course in learning how to fly a crop dusting plane at the University of Minnesota's Crookston campus, which is affiliated with the University of North Dakota's renown flying program, where Guess received his degree. Guess and Moussaoui are about the same age. That might even explain why he gave Moussaoui unattended access to a computer program on flying a 747 jumbo jet at the Eagan Flight School where Guess was working while Moussaoui was a student there.

One of Eagan's ex-managers, who prefers to remain unnamed, told reporters that Guess had placed a CD-ROM containing the 747 software at a work station in advance of one of Moussaoui's training sessions, before his flight instructor arrived. After Moussaoui was arrested, the FBI found the software program copied on his laptop computer. Now, keep in mind that Guess had been a victim of layoffs at the flight academy where he had worked prior to this. He needed money. Moussaoui needed the software.

We are not maintaining that one or both of the pilots were bribed or otherwise encouraged to make sure the fatal flight was not canceled. (In spite of Conry's apparent nervousness about the flight and his preliminary efforts to cancel it, that can be interpreted as concern about the weather.) Nor are we intimating that one or more of the pilots was paid to secretly carry a mysterious package onto the plane. Nor are we suggesting they were following some kind of order to be compensated financially to fly over a certain area. Nor are we suggesting that one or both of the pilots were motivated for some reason to be part of a "suicide flight," like the plan Moussaoui and the terrorists had planned for 9/11.

We are only stating that the NTSB's use of a pilot's criminal record to demonstrate "pilot error" the way NTSB has done seems to be barking up the wrong tree. What if, however, they had more broadly defined the concept to include possible errors that they made via their involvement in a conspiracy to kill Senator Wellstone? We know that both pilots were in serious financial difficulties. Guess had been laid off from another job and was over his head with expenses. Conry, according to the NTSB report by Bramble, said the Conrys were performing a major renovation of their home, had just spent nearly

$7,500 dollars in flight certification costs, and that his wife said that they had financial challenges "because he was not making the same money as a pilot as when he was a nurse and she had worked full-time in September 2002 to help out."

It would be unfair not to mention other reasons that the NTSB concluded that the pilots were incompetent, besides Conry's conviction. For example, in addition to Conry's felony conviction, some pilots told the NTSB human performance investigator, William Bramble, that some copilots said Conry was not particularly assertive. In his report, however, Bramble also said "other copilots said they thought Conry could be assertive if necessary." Assertiveness, of course, can be rather subjective to assess.

The NTSB said some copilots said Conry rarely flew when they were paired with him and this made them uncertain of his skill level. One pilot expressed concerns about his flying skills and potential for distraction. Conry failed the practical test for his Airline Transport Pilot Certificate in 1989, but he received additional training and passed the test on August 4, 1989. Conry falsified his medical form by denying that he had a waiver for defective distant vision, but he submitted to a comprehensive eye exam in 1990 and passed. He also did not acknowledge a 1990 felony conviction on a medical application form he submitted on August 11, 1992. During the eventful flight, at takeoff Conry had activated the auto pilot switch instead of the yaw damper switch, causing the aircraft to pitch down. The copilot corrected the problem. Also on that day Conry repeatedly said his call sign was "Citation 6356K" instead of "King Air 6356K" until a controller corrected him and he acknowledge the error and apologized.

The NTSB's basis for pilot error was largely determined by Bramble's "Specialist's Factual Report." He spent a total of twelve days interviewing people in person or by telephone to gather the evidence that ultimately was used in the final NTSB report to determine that pilot error was the cause of the Wellstone crash. Since pilot involvement in a possible conspiracy had been automatically discounted, none of the kinds of questions that we have posed here were ever asked.

Weather observations at EVM [Eveleth Virginia Airport] are made by an AWOS [Automatic Weather Observation Service], 38 which is located about 2 miles northwest of the accident site at an elevation of about 1,380 feet. Observations from this station are reported every 20 minutes. At 10:14 on the day of the accident, the AWOS reported that the visibility was 3 statute miles in light snow and that the sky condition was scattered clouds at 400 feet and overcast at 700 feet. At 1034, the AWOS reported that the visibility was 4 statute miles in mist and that the sky condition was overcast at 400 feet. Both AWOS reports indicated calm winds and temperatures of 1° C.

The Hibbing, Minnesota, ASOS [Automated Surface Observing System], which is located about 16 miles west of the accident site at an elevation of 1,351 feet, provides high-resolution data that is recorded every 5 minutes. At 1005 on the day of the accident, the ASOS reported that the visibility was about 3 statute miles in mist and that the sky condition was overcast at 500 feet. At 1025, the ASOS reported that the visibility was 4 statute miles in mist and that the sky condition was overcast at 300 feet.

Recall that Gary Ulman said it was cold and a bit icy at the time of his flight search, which he considered to be perfectly normal for northern Minnesota. He said, the weather was even better than the official flight forecast. The clouds were higher and the visibility was twice the reported two miles.

EVM's assistant airport manager stated that, when he was looking for the crash site from the air, he was flying at 1,800 feet (that is, about 420 feet agl), and he never entered the clouds. He stated that the AWOS (which was reporting a 700-foot overcast ceiling) seemed to be reporting correctly because the cloud tops appeared to be about 200 to 300 feet above his airplane. He added that the cloud bases were somewhat ragged and variable in height. He stated that he could see landmarks on the ground up to 4 to 5 miles away.

AIR TRAFFIC CONTROL

The Duluth ATCT [Airport Traffic Control Tower] has three radar positions: approach control south, approach control north, and approach control local. At the time of the accident,

all of the radar positions were combined at the approach control south workstation, which is located in the facility's radar
room. The approach control south radar controller was
responsible for airspace within a 30-mile radius of DLH [Duluth
International Airport] from the surface to 12,000 feet and for
airspace that extended 20 miles northwest of Hibbing,
Minnesota, from the surface to 8,000 feet; EVM lies within this
area of airspace. The DLH approach control south radar controller began working for the FAA on December 2, 1984, and
was assigned to the Duluth ATCT on March 21, 1985. He
became fully certified at the Duluth ATCT on February 27, 1987.
The DLH approach control south radar controller stated that at
the time he was handling the accident airplane, the range of
his radar display was set at 60 miles. He stated that he remembered observing the accident airplane's radar target
intercepting the final approach course about 9 miles from the
runway threshold and that it appeared to him that the radar
target was aligned correctly on final approach at a steady 3,500
feet.

The report admits that the error bands for these
calculations could not be determined with certainty, but in any case
all this indicates is that things were going smoothly with the flight at
this point.

The majority of the airplane sustained severe damage
consistent with impact forces and/or postimpact fire. Several of
the airplane's systems, including the stall warning and deicing
systems, were too damaged by post impact fire and impact
forces to determine their preimpact configuration and oper-
ability.

The high maintenance standard for this plane, however, would
support the inference that they were working properly. It is interesting they are leaving the impression that the condition of these safety
systems prior to the crash was unknown based on evidence available
after the crash.

To emphasize the importance of the point about the nature of the
fire, note the description of class "C" fires provided by the National
Fire Protection Association:

C. Class C-class "C" fires are those associated with electricity or electronic equipment. The primary extinguishing agent is CO2, but high-velocity fog may also be used as a last resort. Foam should not be used as it will damage the equipment and may present a shock hazard. Solid water stream should never be used. If at all possible, the equipment should first be de-energized. Blue-white smoke.

This provides circumstantial evidence that there may have been an electrical fire aboard the plane, perhaps even prior to the crash. The NTSB report continues:

> Handheld tape measurements, survey data, and aerial observations indicated that the airplane descended through the trees wings level and upright on about a 26° downward flight path angle on a ground track of about 180°.

This angle is too steep to suggest anything but a very serious dive, not one likely to result from a low altitude stall even, but from a plane completely out of control very abruptly or all of a sudden. This would have seemed important enough to emphasize.

> The majority of the wreckage, which consisted of the forward fuselage, the cockpit, and most of the wings, was found at the southern end of the main wreckage field. None of these components exhibited evidence of in-flight fire or preimpact structural damage. The right elevator was found attached to the stabilizer and exhibited severe impact and fire damage.

It would seem impossible to know from the wreckage, especially when it had burned for hours, whether an in-flight fire had started or not. Recall that witnesses saw a flash of light while the plane was in the sky, whose testimony was disregarded in the NTSB's report and who were not allowed to comment at any public hearings.

> Sections of both wings were recovered and exhibited postimpact fire damage. The flap actuators were recovered. (According to Raytheon documentation, the measurements taken of the flap actuators were consistent with the flaps being in the approach position [about 30 percent] at the time of the accident.)

In one rare AP photo, one wing is in the foreground. It was charred, though the tree next to it was not. Had it been moved? In any case, neither wing was destroyed by fire as was the fuselage. Since the fuel tanks were in the wings and the fuel would have burned black smoke not blue, then we could surmise that the fire was an electrical fire caused by something that affected the electrical system, an idea we develop in the last chapter. As for photos, it is interesting to note here that the first responders on the scene were ordered not to take any photos of the wreckage by the FBI. Why? Even the *Associated Press* photographer (who asked us not to name him) had a very difficult time getting photos. He reported to us that he was only allowed fifteen minutes at the crash site, something he found very, very unusual. Behind the protection of his anonyminity, he was able to state frankly to us that he had serious suspicions about the "accident."

> The cockpit instrument panel was extensively damaged by postimpact fire, and all of the instruments were found set-tled into a large pile under the cockpit window frame. Several of the instruments were recovered and transported to the Safety Board's Materials Laboratory for further examination. Several of the cockpit instruments were too damaged to war-rant further examination. The left-side airspeed indicator's case was severely burned, melted, and distorted, and the indicator's data plate was missing. All of the exterior markings and paint were burned off, and the glass face was broken and discolored. The dial assembly was found attached to the mechanism assembly and had distinct blackened areas on it, one of which was located directly above a small screw that is above the 100-knots-airspeed mark.

Several instruments were recovered. We wonder if this plane was equipped with a voice recorder and if it was removed. As stated earlier, the head NTSB investigator, Carol Carmody, a former employee of the CIA, was looking for it, not knowing that one is not required on a King-Air 100 because it can be legally flown by only one pilot. But what if one had been installed by the FBI, the CIA, or the Capitol Police since they knew a U.S. senator would be traveling in it? What if they removed it?

A fuel-fed fire erupted after the airplane impacted the ground.

The fuels used by this particular airplane would burn with coarse black and not bluish-white smoke. (Those fuels by technical name are JP-4, JP-5 (MIL-T-5624); JP-8 (MIL-T-83133); JET A, JET A-1; and JET B. There would have been a maximum of 115 total usable gallons in the nacelle tanks and a maximum of 258 total useable gallons in the wing tanks.)

> According to the Saint Louis County Medical Examiner's autopsy reports, the cause of death for the pilot, copilot, and all of the passengers was multiple traumatic injuries sustained during impact. Three of the individuals showed evidence of post impact smoke and soot inhalation.

Why did the autopsy take much longer than initially predicted? At least an autopsy was conducted, unlike some other important cases, including when Secretary Ron Brown's plane crashed. But it took weeks not several days as was announced. Why?

> The Safety Board conducted an airplane performance study to establish a history of the accident airplane's motions and the pilot's actions. As stated in section 1.1, radar data from the last two recorded radar returns indicate that the accident airplane had slowed to about 76 KCAS (calibrated airspeed) at 1,800 feet. The Raytheon King Air A100 AFM and Raytheon calculations indicate that the wings-level, gear-down stall speed, assuming an estimated landing weight of about 10,500 pounds with the flaps in the approach setting, would have been about 77 calibrated airspeed with the power at flight idle.

Radar readings under 2,500 feet, however, are not sufficiently accurate to conclude for certain the speed of the plane. To conclude that the one knot under proves the plane stalled is not a reliable conclusion, although it ought to be obvious that any plane would pass through its "stall speed", if it were in the process of crashing.

> The tests conducted without simulated airframe icing showed that the flight path and speed of the accident airplane, as indicated by the radar data, could be reasonably matched making minor pitch control inputs and engine power reductions. The stall warning occurred during these tests between 81 and 84 KCAS. During the tests, increasing the power quickly resulted in an increase in airspeed and no further stall warnings.

FAILURE OF NTSB'S OWN CRASH SIMULATIONS

The NTSB sought to prove the credibility of its explanation for the crash by simulating the stall with a simulator for a similar aircraft.

This followed standard NTSB procedure. Significantly, the NTSB couldn't get the simulated aircraft to stall the way they claimed Wellstone's plane had.

> According to Raytheon and FSI, no known King Air A100 simulators exist. The Airplane Performance Group chose the King Air C90B model for simulations because it has a similar configuration and stall speeds to the A100 model; however, it is not fully certified to replicate the A100's flight characteristics.

The NTSB accused Conry and Guess of not watching the plane's indicators. "One of them should have been monitoring the instruments," said Bill Bramble, a human performance investigator for the NTSB. Still, NTSB board member Richard Healing called the conclusion that this had caused the crash "speculative," pointing out that the report did not say how the pilots missed the red flags or why they failed to make adjustments. "We don't know why," Healing acknowledged. "It's quite speculative."

This conclusion was especially disturbing, since the NTSB's own simulations flew a plane at abnormally slow speeds but still were unable to bring it down. That by itself should have forced consideration of other possible causes that would probably have lead in the direction of sabotage, as we shall consider below.

Even if the pilots had neglected to check their airspeed and altitude, it should have been possible for them to increase power and regain altitude. The stall warning on a King Air is quite loud. With two pilots (remember only one is needed to fly this aircraft) and six passengers, it could not have been missed. There should have been ample time to regain speed. This consideration becomes very important in evaluating alternative hypotheses about whether this crash was brought about by accident or by design.

Although the U-21 has cockpit controls and displays similar to the A100, it is not certified to fully replicate the A100's flight characteristics. A simulation was flown to duplicate the descent profile and ground track of the accident flight. Investigators noted that when the pilots were attempting to maintain a low-descent rate at a low-torque setting (about 400 foot-pounds [ft-lbs]) with the airspeed lower than 100 knots, a gradual, significant pitchup was necessary to maintain altitude. The stall warning horn sounded when the airplane was at 82 knots.

> Specific stall recovery initiation procedures, including how to respond if the stall warning horn sounds in flight, were not noted in any of Aviation Charter's manuals. However, one Aviation Charter copilot stated that during company flight training, she was instructed to initiate stall recovery when the stall warning horn sounded. Further, a Quick Turn instructor indicated that because the flight-training device was not a motion-based device, pilots were expected to initiate stall recovery when the stall warning horn sounded.

Our critics on the internet have tried to discount the NTSB's own simulations, on the grounds that they were not conducted under exactly the same conditions. But doing that would require using the original pilots, plane, and weather. Being exact is obviously impossible, which suggests a standard of evidence that could never be satisfied. It is safe to assume that the simulations by the NTSB are close enough to support the inference that the crash was probably not caused by the pilots, the plane, or the weather, which means we have to search elsewhere.

Further, we find it rather difficult to believe that any remotely qualified pilot would not be aware of and knowledgeable that the function of a stall warning is to warn of a stall. The *Maneuvers Guide* contains guidelines to determine acceptable pilot performance during training of the stall recovery maneuver. According to the *Maneuvers Guide,* a pilot's performance of the stall recovery maneuver requires that at least the following conditions be met:

> *a. Exhibits adequate knowledge of the factors, which influence stall characteristics, including the use of various drag configurations, power settings, pitch attitudes, weights, and bank angles. Also, exhibits adequate knowledge of the proper procedure for resuming normal flight.*

> *e. Initiates recovery [from stall] at the first indication of buffeting, decay of control effectiveness, other cues related to specific aircraft design characteristics, or as directed by the instructor.*

> *f. Recovers to a reference airspeed, altitude and heading, allowing only the acceptable altitude, airspeed, heading loss, or deviation.*

According to Aviation Charter's chief pilot, moreover, who

conducted most of Aviation Charter's King Air flight training, company pilots were taught SOPs during ground and flight instruction and were expected to use them. They should have known what to do.

> The flight crew members were properly certificated and had received the training for pilot certification prescribed by Federal regulations. No evidence indicated any preexisting medical or other physical condition that might have adversely affected the flight crew's performance during the accident flight. Fatigue most likely did not degrade the performance of either pilot on the day of the accident. Therefore, the Safety Board could not determine who was flying the airplane at the time of the accident.

One might well ask, *then why is so much made about the incompetence of the pilot, especially when we were told by NTSB that he often let copilots fly?* Jeff Blodgett, Wellstone's campaign manager, was absolutely certain in conversation with Four Arrows that Conry's incompetence was the sole reason for the alleged pilot errors that are supposed to have brought the plane down. The answer is of course that he believes both pilots were incompetent so it does not matter which one was flying. But there is nothing here to suggest that either pilot was less than fully qualified to fly this plane. The NTSB's own report does not support its conclusion of pilot incompetence.

> As discussed in section 1.5.1.2, there were numerous discrepancies with the pilot logbooks that called into question the accuracy of his flight time record-keeping.

However, the investigation found no evidence indicating that the pilot lacked the required flight time or that these discrepancies in the logbooks were related to the cause of this accident. Again there is nothing here to support pilot's incompetence.

FLIGHT CREW'S INADEQUATE APPROACH SETUP

> Shortly after 1018:31, as the airplane approached the published EVM VOR [Very high frequency Omni Range frequency] runway 27 final approach course from the south at about 164 KCAS and decreasing, ATC instructed the flight crew to turn left to a heading of 300° until established on the final approach

course. However, the flight crew overshot the approach course almost immediately after being issued the turn, and the airplane ultimately traveled for almost 1 mile north of the course as it continued the turn toward the course until establishing a ground track of about 262°.

We have already observed that it was not uncommon to overshoot this exact turning point and we know the plane adequately compensated for it and lined up. This part of the NTSB report just makes it sound as though the pilot had done something terrible by overshooting the approach course relative to not making the turn exactly when control said they should. This does not necessarily imply anything about the cause of the crash or pilot competence, since we know that overshoots were common.

The airplane began its descent from 3,500 1019:20. The airplane should have been at 130 knots at the start of the descent with flaps at the approach setting and the landing gear down. Because the airplane was fast at this point in the approach, the flight crew had to lose a significant amount of airspeed and altitude in a short amount of time. As the airplane descended through 3,200 feet, its airspeed and vertical speed peaked at about 170 KCAS and 1,400 fpm, respectively.

Losing the airspeed and altitude at this altitude was not an issue and the difference between 160 knots and 130 knots at this point would not have been a significant difference. Which raises questions as to why the official report suggests otherwise. They appear to be related to the presumptive non-response to the stall warning in a situation where the stall alarm ought to have allowed for them to regain control.

When the airplane was approximately 4 miles from the runway threshold, it was still at 2,300 feet and about 160 KCAS; however, at this point in the approach, the airplane still should have been at an airspeed of about 130 knots. Further, Aviation Charter's chief pilot stated that the landing gear should be extended when the flight crew starts the descent to the MDA and that the power should simultaneously be reduced to get down to approach speed. However, the maximum speed for landing gear extension is 156 knots. The airspeed exceeded 156 knots when the airplane started its descent to the MDA and during most of the descent. The chief pilot and other Aviation Charter pilots indicated that it would have been difficult to exceed 156 knots with the gear extended. Therefore, it appears that the flight crew did not properly configure the airplane at the start of the approach (extending the landing gear or reducing power before descending from 3,500 feet).

Yet at least one of the witnesses said the landing gear was down. Furthermore the difference between 160 and 156 knots should not have been significant. Lowering the landing gear below 3,500 feet should not have been a significant problem, either. According to Aviation Charter's chief pilot, the company instructed its pilots to fly nonprecision approaches at 130 knots until short final and to cross the runway threshold and touch down at 100 knots. We cannot be sure from what we know that the speed monitoring at this altitude was sufficiently accurate to say what speed the plane was traveling prior to the crash. The needle, in spite of the melted instrument panel, was pointing at 196 knots, which presumably indicated the speed upon impact.

FLIGHT CREW'S FAILURE TO STABILIZE THE APPROACH

At 1020:36, the airplane's airspeed was about 156 knots about 3.7 miles from the runway 27 threshold and it was descending through about 2,200 feet. At 1020:54, when the airplane was 3 miles from the runway threshold, it was descending through about 2,100 feet and slowing through about 130 KCAS. The last two radar returns indicate that the airplane was at approximately 1,800 feet and slowing through about 76 KCAS, which is the approximate stall speed for the configuration in which the airplane was found after the accident. The last radar return was about 2 miles southeast of the runway threshold.

Airplane simulations showed (and the stall warning system design indicates) that the flight crew should have received at least several seconds of aural stall warning in the cockpit if the airspeed decreased below 81 to 84 knots, if the stall warning system was working properly, and if the airplane was not affected by ice accumulation. The flight crew should have had other indications of low airspeed, moreover, such as increased pitch attitude and a quieter slipstream, and might have experienced buffeting and less responsive flight controls, depending on the airspeed and whether there was any ice accumulation. Since the airplane was apparently not equipped with a CVR, because of the approximate nature of the airspeed calculations, and because airplane maneuvering or small amounts of ice accumulation can increase an airplane's stall speed, the Safety Board was not able to determine when or whether the stall warning horn activated on the accident flight or if buffeting or loss of flight control effectiveness occurred. But the absence of certain knowledge does not affect the probability that the stall warning horn was properly functional.

> It is clear that the flight crew failed to monitor the airplane's airspeed and allowed it to decrease to a dangerously low level (as low as about 50 knots below the company's recommended approach airspeed) and to remain below the recommended approach airspeed for about 50 seconds. Further, the flight crew failed to recognize that a stall was imminent. In sum, the Safety Board concludes that the flight crew failed to maintain an appropriate course and speed for the approach and did not properly configure the airplane at the start of the approach, making the later stages of the approach more difficult. Further, the Safety Board concludes that, during the later stages of the approach, the flight crew failed to monitor the airplane's airspeed and allowed it to decrease to a dangerously low level (as low as about 50 knots below the company's recommended approach airspeed) and to remain below the recommended approach airspeed for about 50 seconds. The Board further concludes that the flight crew failed to recognize that a stall was imminent and allowed the airplane to enter a stall from which they did not recover.

Again, between the stall warning and the improbability that the crew would not have known a stall was imminent, the inaccuracies of determining air speeds below 2500 feet, the estimated air speed of the plane being so close to the acceptable air speed for preventing a stall, make this conclusion overly simplistic. Even more importantly, it assumes that the pilots were able to control the aircraft. Consider the alternative, namely: the plane lost airspeed and altitude because they were unable to control it.

The Board also concludes that the inadequate airspeed or the full CDI needle deflection should have prompted the flight crew to execute a go-around; however, they failed to do so.

Then we must wonder why the plane crashed while going in the opposite direction of the runway approach. It would appear they were attempting to execute a go-around. Or...

The last two recorded radar returns indicate that the airplane was at approximately 1,800 feet and within 2 miles of the runway 27 threshold. Further, a witness indicated that he saw the accident airplane just beneath a low layer of clouds. Therefore, because the airplane was most likely in and out of the clouds before the accident, the Safety Board concludes that clouds might have prevented the flight crew from seeing the airport.

We saw earlier that weather reports showed that visibility was three miles.

The airplane was most likely not in the cloud layer in which moderate icing was present for enough time to accumulate any significant airframe icing. Further, any icing that the airplane might have accumulated would have been shed by the deicing equipment, or it would have begun shedding off the airplane's surfaces as it was descending through 5,000 feet because of the warming temperatures. In addition, the airplane's performance was not consistent with the effects of icing, and flight simulations showed that the performance could be matched with and without simulated icing with enough reserve engine power available to increase the airspeed during the descent. Therefore, the Safety Board concludes that icing did not affect the airplane's performance during the descent.

Multiple concurrent tasks would have required efficient coordination between the two crewmembers; however, as concluded previously, the flight crew likely was not effectively applying CRM [Crew Resource Management] techniques during the approach segment of the flight. Therefore, these tasks likely were not being effectively handled during the approach. Further, the Safety Board's investigation revealed that the pilots often performed poorly when flying approaches.

Yet in Bramble's own NTSB report of February 20, 2003, he reports that Guess and Conry enjoyed a good flying partnership with no known complaints. Although some newspapers reported that there had been some complaints by other pilots or instructors about problems with flying approaches, these were not included in Bramble's report and the certifications and experience of the pilots. (Conry himself had owned five planes of his own during his life.) and their certifications would not support such a conclusion. The NTSB seems to be neglecting its own evidence.

> Current Federal airworthiness standards require that airplanes be equipped to provide a clear and distinctive stall warning to the flight crew at a speed that is at least 5 knots higher than stall speed. However, stall warnings do not always provide flight crews with timely notification of developing hazardous low-airspeed conditions. For example, abrupt maneuvering can increase angle-of-attack so rapidly that a stall could occur nearly simultaneously with the stall warning, and ice accumulation, which raises the stall speed, could degrade the stall warning margin to the point at which little or no stall warning is provided.

Why is the NTSB referring to ice accumulation here when they have already clearly established that icing was not a problem? The accident airplane was equipped with a stall warning system designed to sound a horn in the cockpit 5-8 knots before the actual stall speed of the airplane in any configuration. In a performance worthy of note, the NTSB is taking a remote possibility and treating it as a probability or even as an actuality. We already knew that the plane lost altitude, airspeed, and crashed.

> In addition, the Board has investigated other events in which the drag associated with airframe ice and pilot inattention led to a critical loss of airspeed. Failure to maintain airspeed during these flights resulted in catastrophic and other unsafe circumstances, such as loss of control, impact with terrain or water, hard landings, and tail strikes.

Once again, the NTSB is rationalizing why the pilots did not heed the warning system by appealing to the presence of ice, which it already dismissed as not being a factor.

> Probable Cause

The National Transportation Safety Board determines that the probable cause of this accident was the flight crew's failure to maintain adequate airspeed, which led to an aerodynamic stall from which they did not recover.

Signed by

ELLEN G. ENGLEMAN Chairman

CAROL J. CARMODY Member

MARK V. ROSENKER Vice Chairman

JOHN J. GOGLIA Member

RICHARD F. HEALING Member

Adopted: November 18, 2003

Let's look at the backgrounds of "Chairman" Ellen Engleman and Vice Chairman Mark Rosenker. Both were directly nominated by George W. Both are public relations professionals. Engleman worked on the Homeland Security team and Rosenker is director of White House military team. Not exactly the kind of people who rock the boat and question the party line.

John Goglia has served as a Member of the National Transportation Safety Board since August 1995. With more than 30 years experience in the aviation industry, he is the first Board Member to hold an FAA aircraft mechanic's certificate. Of the five members of the Board, he stands alone as the one aircraft and aviation expert.

The following is from a speech that he gave, which we found at http://www.ntsb.gov/speeches/JG960628.htm :

> *Unless the accident is caused by a terrorist act, the NTSB is in charge of the investigation. They secure the site in order to protect evidence, and interview witnesses. They ensure that the facts become known, and work to uncover the cause of the accident.*
>
> *At this stage of the investigation, lawyers are not allowed at the crash site.*

*In cases where terrorism is suspected, the accident site is initially consid-
ered a crime scene, and the FBI is in charge. the NTSB will assist as
requested in this effort.*

*The length of time the "go-team" remains on the scene varies with need,
but generally a team completes its on-scene work in seven to ten days. The
Safety Board remains in charge of the accident site until it determines the
site is no longer critical to its investigation."*

What we learn here is, first, that the primary qualifications valued
for membership in the NTSB concern public relations and political
connections, not technical knowledge or engineering skills. Second,
that, when a bona-fide expert on air crashes speaks his mind, what he
tells us about how air crashes are supposed to be handled contradicts
what happened here. Both are profoundly disturbing because they
confirm our worst suspicions about the potential for the NTSB to
cover up the true causes of a crash, with or without the assistance of
the FBI.

ADDITIONAL NTSB REPORT NOTES

The National Transportation Safety Board learned about
the accident about 1130 on October 25, 2002. A go-team was
assembled, and it departed that same day and arrived on
scene about 2045 that evening. Accompanying the team was
Acting Chairman Carol J. Carmody and representatives from the
Safety Board's Offices of Government, Public, and Family Affairs.

Parties to the investigation were the Federal Aviation
Administration; Aviation Charter, Inc.; Raytheon Aircraft
Company; and Hartzell Propeller, Inc. An accredited representative from the Transportation Safety Board of Canada and a
technical advisor from Pratt & Whitney Canada also assisted in
the investigation.

Notice the FBI and the U.S. Capitol Police are not listed as
parties to the investigation. If they were not party to the investigation, as the NTSB claimed to us on the phone, why did
Minneapolis-based FBI agent Paul McCabe say that about 15
agents with the Bureau's Evidence Response Team would be

assisting NTSB investigators? McCabe emphasized through the FBI has no reason to suspect foul play caused the airplane crash. "This is a normal procedure. It's a precautionary move. We will be assisting the NTSB on their investigation. They will be the lead agency on this investigation. I have received a number of phone calls from reporters with questions about terrorism. Currently what I can tell you is there is no indication, nor is there is any intelligence information that would suggest that the crash of Senator Wellstone's plane was in any way related to an act of terrorism," according to the FBI spokesman.

Public Hearing

No public hearing was held for this accident.

A public meeting, called a "Sunshine meeting", is ordinarily held in a case like this in accordance with the following NTSB policy:

PURPOSE

The National Transportation Safety Board conducts public hearings for the purpose of supplementing the facts discovered during the on-scene and subsequent follow-up investigation of the accident. Public hearings generally are held with regard to a major accident in which there is wide and sustained public interest, or significant safety issues. Testimony is obtained through public hearings to ensure an accurate, complete and well-documented factual record. The Safety Board is a public agency, and conducts its investigations in a public manner. A public hearing enables the Safety Board to meet its mandate to conduct in-depth objective accident investigations, without bias or undue influence from industry or other government agencies. It is an exercise in accountability: accountability that the Safety Board is conducting a thorough and fair investigation and accountability on the part of industry and other government agencies that they are fulfilling their responsibilities.

To not have a public meeting for this crash obviously violates the public meeting rationale. The lip service to "accountability" paid above only serves to further expose the

NTSB's own hypocrisy. A possible explanation is that the Rand Corporation recently found that the NTSB staff was "overworked."

Sherman H. Skolnick has advanced another theory some may find more plausible. Since 1963, Skolnick has been the founder and chairman of Citizen's Committee to Clean Up the Courts, a public interest group researching and disclosing certain instances of judicial bribery and political murders. In 1973, Mr. Skolnick wrote *The Secret History of Airplane Sabotage,* a heavily documented book dealing with, among other things, a sabotaged plane crash in Chicago in December 1972, a month after Nixon was re-elected President. Twelve Watergate figures died when a United Air Lines plane pancaked just short of Midway airport. The NTSB investigated.

Among the dead in the crash zone were Mrs. E. Howard Hunt, wife of the Watergate burglar, and others linked to the Watergate Affair. According to Skolnick, Ms. Hunt had over two million dollars in valuables, obtained by blackmailing Nixon over his role in the 1963 political assassination of President John F. Kennedy. Skolnick's group "liberated" the entire unpublicized file of the NTSB, some 1,300 pages of documented reports and pictures that indicated sabotage. Skolnick also brought a suit against the NTSB with accusations of cover-up. The NTSB re-opened its public hearings on the crash but continued to contend it was caused by "pilot error". In the chapter that follows, we shall consider whether the Wellstone crash was caused by a similar "pilot error."

CHAPTER SEVEN

HOW IT WAS DONE

I'm for the little fellers, not the Rockefellers.

—Senator Paul Wellstone

In Chapter 5, we proposed that electromagnetic weaponry may have been responsible for the crash of the King Air. In this chapter, we demonstrate the credibility of this alternative. If the NTSB had done an honest and thorough investigation of the crash, it might well have concluded that an EMP was the most likely explanation.

However, if the only alternatives that are given consideration are that the crash was due to (h1) the plane, (h2) the weather, or (h3) the pilots, then if the plane was not the problem and the weather was not that bad, then a simple argument by elimination—it was not (h1) and was not (h2); therefore, it must have been (h3)—would dictate the conclusion that ought to be drawn. In this case, however, the evidence indicates that the pilots were appropriately qualified— where Conry passed his FAA "flight check" only days prior to the fatal flight—which makes that inference more difficult to accept, especially when the range of alternatives is constrained.

The NTSB did not give any consideration at all to the possibility that the crash might have been brought about by design rather than by accident. The early arrival of the FBI was not only extremely suspicious on its own, but afforded an occasion for "cleaning up" what may have been a crime scene rather than the scene of an accident. If only the only alternatives given consideration—such as the plane, the weather, and the pilots—are compatible with an accident, then that the event happened as the consequence of an accident becomes a logical necessity. Only by taking into account additional alternatives—such as a small bomb, a gas canister, or an electromagnetic weapon, for example—does assassination become a possibility.

The NTSB's conclusion that the pilots were at fault and brought about a crash by failing to pay attention to their altitude and flight speed, when considered on its own, sounds at least faintly ridiculous. Paying attention to altitude and flight speed, after all, are the most basic elements of flight training. Any pilot who failed to pay attention to his altitude and flight speed would thereby have demonstrated his incompetence. Given their background and training, it is not probable that Conry or Guess were incompetent pilots. Indeed, by the FAA's own standards, they were both competent. The probability that a single competent pilot would fail to monitor altitude and airspeed, especially during a landing for a duration sufficient to bring about a crash, is extremely small. If it occurred as often as once in a hundred, plane crashes would be ubiquitous.

Moreover, since there were *two* qualified pilots, if we assume that a qualified pilot would only neglect his altitude and airspeed, say, one time in a hundred, the probability that two qualified pilots would both commit this blunder together would be no more than one in ten thousand. So even coarse calculations based on exaggerated probabilities for performance failures of the kind attributed here suggest that the NTSB's account should not be taken seriously. But that requires considering alternatives according to which the reason why two competent pilots did not maintain control of their aircraft is not because they were able to control the plane and neglected to do so, as the NTSB's report suggests, but that the plane came down, even though they were performing these tasks properly, because they no longer had control the plane, due to abnormal and unexpected circumstances.

When you factor in the stall warning system, moreover, it becomes even more preposterous to assume that two competent pilots would neglect their altitude or airspeeds, and then ignore a loud stall warning alert. The NTSB report suggests that the plane might have lost altitude so abruptly that there would have been no time to respond to the warning, which could have occurred concurrent with the stall it was designed to warn against. But there is no evidence that supports this possibility. The probability that two competent pilots would ignore their airspeed and altitude when the plane was within their control in the absence of some abnormal and unexpected conditions must have a value that approaches or even equals zero.

There are historical precedents, of course, for a government investigation to accept conclusions that were contradicted by its own evidence. In her book on the death of John F. Kennedy, *Accessories after the Fact* (1967), Sylvia Meagher demonstrated that the conclusions drawn in *The Warren Report* (1964) were contradicted by the evidence, documents, and records in its 26 volumes of so-called "supporting evidence". The NTSB's performance appears to be on a par with the conclusion that Lee Oswald shot JFK, even though witnesses saw him in and around the lunchroom on the 2nd floor at the time of the shooting, his wife said he admired President Kennedy, and the carbine he was supposed to have used was not even a high-velocity weapon. Neither account is credible; nevertheless, the government, no doubt, will continue to defend both of them.

ALTERNATIVE EXPLANATIONS

The most plausible alternative explanations relative to the Wellstone crash include the use of a small bomb, a gas canister, a high-tech weapon, such as an electromagnetic pulse (EMP) device, or some combination. These alternatives imply that the crash was deliberate rather than accidental. When assassination is excluded from consideration, as in the case of the NTSB, then no investigation could possibly yield assassination as the explanation, even when it happens to be true. When there are three versions of the accident hypothesis (the pilots, the plane, or the weather was at fault) and at least three versions of the non-accident/assassination hypothesis (a small bomb, a gas canister, or some new high-tech weapon was the cause), then if the assassination alternatives are not given consideration, it becomes logically impossible to derive any of them as having been the cause of the crash—not as a result of systematic and objective scientific investigation but as the result of a preliminary and no doubt political decision "not to go there". Evidence suggests that is what was done in this case.

Moreover, recent changes to the law empower the Attorney General to make a decision as to whether or not a crash scene might involve "criminal activity". In that case, the NTSB will surrender its lead on a transportation incident, but otherwise not. This makes the

Attorney General the arbiter of whether or not an event, such as a plane crash, formally even qualifies for a criminal investigation (www.ntsb.gov/Abt_NTSB/invest.htm). Some might think that this means that a corrupt administration could take advantage of the law by using a compliant, not to say complicit, Attorney General to decline to declare the possibility of any criminal activity. That might compel the NTSB to restrict any investigation to only accidental causes rather than deliberate ones, thereby covering things up. It is also interesting to note that, as a matter of formal policy, NTSB determinations of probable cause "cannot be entered as evidence into a court of law." Incredible.

What this means is that, when there is a puzzling situation of the very kind we are discussing, if the Attorney General does not identify the crash site as one in which "the accident may have been caused by an intentional criminal act"—that is, as one in which the incident was "no accident"—then it is apparently not open to criminal investigation. Which offers all the more reason why anyone puzzled by a situation of this kind may have to take matters into their own hand. How can we possibly know whether or not the NTSB report on the death of Paul Wellstone is or is not remotely plausible if we have not undertaken an independent investigation of the incident that considers all the alternatives in relation to all of the evidence?

Indeed, there were multiple concerns that prompted Jim Fetzer to begin his own study of this case. Considerations of the role of motive, means, and opportunity strongly suggested that those who benefited the most from this event were the Republicans—not your average G.O.P. voter, of course—but the Bush administration. And within the administration itself, the most plausible candidates appear be the troika which runs things, Dick Cheney, Karl Rove, and Donald Rumsfeld. Chapter Two has explained that the political motives for taking him out were overwhelming, as a consequence of which he was viewed as "a hunted man". Because he was a public servant whose activities and schedule were widely known, it would not be difficult to find a time and a place to take him out, especially as the political consequences of his demise became more desirable. Which of course is why, if there were a plan to assassinate a United States Senator, it would be prudent to wait until the necessity for doing so was clear, say, as he was pulling away around ten days before election.

As in the case of President Kennedy, killing Senator Wellstone would not pose the principal problem. Rather, the onus was on covering it up so that the hit itself did not become a factor in the election. It would be essential to create a situation where his death could be cast as an "accident" rather than stir up suspicion that a corrupt administration had once again exercised its power to defeat democracy. That would not be a helpful platform to promote Republican ascendancy in the Senate, even if it were the grim reality. So the use of an airplane crash as the means must have been appealing, especially when the legal ramifications of the situation were so easily controlled. It would be best if the crime could be committed in a relatively remote area where there would be few civilian spectators. The FBI could move in quickly and control the scene, declaim the absence of any indications of "terrorist activity"—which can be said with a straight face, if there has been no investigation at all, since then there are "at this time" no indications of the cause of the crash at all and therefore no indications of "criminal activity", terrorist or not.

The temptations of a "fool proof" approach of this kind may have been virtually irresistible. Thinking about the incident at the time, Jim was struck by the sudden loss of communication simultaneous with loss of control, which had led him to consider weapons that might bring about those effects, such as a small bomb, a gas canister, or an electromagnetic weapon. The autopsy reports indicate that three of the victims had smoke in their lungs, which implied they had survived the moment of impact long enough to be affected by the fire, or that the plane was on fire on the way down. When Jim learned of John Ongaro's cell phone anomaly, that strongly influenced his analysis of the incident, since all of these events—the abrupt loss of control, the cessation of communication, and the odd noise on Ongaro's phone—also appeared to have occurred at just the right time of 10:18 AM in advance of the crash itself about two minutes later. (An acoustical study of weapons of this kind suggests that the kind of sounds Ongaro described would be highly probable in relation his cell phone experience. Such a study has been posted on *www.assassinationscience.com* under "HERF Data #1".) This reconstruction of the incident, alas, implies that the occupants of the plane had to have known that they were going down—and very probably about to die—during that two minute interval.

The set of effects had reminded Jim of those he had read in on-line sources regarding EMP weapons. *Time* (http://www.time.com/time/covers/1101030127/nmicro.html) had reported on the availability of one class of EMP weaponry—high-powered microwave weapons—that were being made available for use in the war in Iraq:

> *HPMs can unleash in a flash as much electrical power—2 billion watts or more— as the Hoover Dam generates in 24 hours. Capacitors aboard the missile discharge an energy pulse—moving at the speed of light and impervious to bad weather—in front of the missile as it nears its target. That pulse can destroy any electronics within 1,000 ft. of the flash by short-circuiting internal electrical connections, thereby wrecking memory chips, ruining computer motherboards and generally screwing up electronic components not built to withstand such powerful surges. It's similar to what can happen to your computer or TV when lightning strikes nearby and a tidal wave of electricity rides in through the wiring.*

We have noted that Attorney Lawrence Judd wrote the NTSB to ask about EMP weapons in the deaths of Wellstone and Carnahan. Robert Benzon, the NTSB head of the investigation and Frank Hilldrup's boss, wrote him back, saying "The NTSB is unaware of any mobile EM force or EM pulse weapon system capable of disabling an aircraft at the ground-to-air ranges that existed in either of the accidents you mention in your email." Benzon's reply does not indicate he is completely unaware of such weapons, only of those that might be capable of doing this particular job. Perhaps he is under strict orders from higher up to offer such a response. Or perhaps he simply knows nothing at all about these weapons, which ought to be of interest to an agency charged with investigating plane crashes.

As we have previously observed, the Carnahan crash and the Wellstone crash bear eerie similarities and differences. The temporal interval between the events and the forthcoming elections was reduced from three weeks down to ten days to allow less time for response. Wellstone's wife, Sheila, was also taken out, so she would be "unavailable" to stand in for him, at Governor Ventura's discretion in Minnesota, similar to the way Mel Carnahan's wife was appointed in his place in Missouri. Indeed, witnesses described a reddish illumination of the sky at the time Mel's plane went down. As in the case of Wellstone, the Carnahan crash took place in a remote region of the state. Unlike Wellstone, the plane was widely scattered. A student of weather has captured an image that occurred at the time of the crash, one which strongly suggests that an electromagnetic weapon might have been involved here (see *assassinationscience.com* under "Wellstone, Carnahan, and JFK, Jr. Anomalies").

Whether or not the NTSB is aware of such weapons, it is unlikely that the United States Capitol Police Dignitary Protection Division does not know about such weapons. At their creation by Congress in 1828, the purpose of the U.S. Capitol Police was to provide security for the U.S. Capitol Building. Today, their mission has expanded to protecting, preventing, detecting, and investigating criminal acts, and protecting Members of Congress, Officers of Congress, and their families throughout entire United States and its territories and possessions.

EMPS IN REAL LIFE

Here are a few abstracts we have derived from unclassified, unlimited distribution references only, yet they describe a variety of beam-weapon systems. For example,

(a) "Defense Technology Plan." *Department of Defense, 1994. This technology plan identifies funding that has been allocated for technologies to be transitioned to new war-fighting involving capabilities that include electronic warfare and directed energy weapons.*

(b) "New World Vistas: Air and Space Power for the 21st Century." *Directed Energy Volume.: Scientific Advisory Board. U.S. Air Force, 1995. Abstract: Directed energy weapons, lasers and microwaves, will have widespread application over the next few decades. A substantial technical data base now allows confident anticipation of weapon applications. Initial airborne weapons capably of destroying or disabling anything that flies—will drive a new warfare paradigm.*

(c) "Review and Prospects of the U.S. Directed-

Energy Weapons Technology Development in 1994." *National Air Intelligence Center 1996. Wright-Patterson AFB. A translation of China Astonautics and Missilery Abstracts (1995). Abstract: Directed-energy weapons are new generation weapons developed on the basis of the new concept of replacing conventional bullets with high energy density beams. Technically, directed-energy weapons can be divided into three branches, namely: (1) laser weapons which can destroy or destabilize targets by using electromagnetic radiation energy beams (2) radio-frequency weapons which can destroy or destabilize targets with radiated electromagnetic energy (3) particle beam weapons which destroy or destabilize targets with neutral high energy atomic partical beams.*

(d) "Trends of Microwave Weapon Development." *National Air Intelligence Center. 1996. Translation of an unidentified Chinese language article. Abstract: Microwave weapons which depend on electric power and are based on electromagnetic pulse technology will replace weapon systems that depend on chemical energy.* By 2001, many directed energy weapons that will appear, including microwave weapons, will have a profound effect on warfare. This article particularly emphasizes the unique role of microwave weapons in countering stealth technology. *[emphasis ours]*

Beyond such article abstracts, a number of books also discuss the properties of these high tech weapons. Two of the better are Angels *Don't Play this HAARP: Advances in Tesla Technology* (1995) and an Australian Air Force publication, *A Doctrine For the Use of Electromagnetic Pulse Bombs* (1993). Dr. Bernard Eastlund, while working for Advanced Power Technologies in the 1980s patented devices that are described as being capable of causing total disruption of communications, missile or aircraft destruction, deflection or confusion and weather modification. These patents were based on the ideas and fundamental research of Nicola Tesla. A number of corporations have appropriated Tesla's work and many of Eastlund's patents were sealed under a U.S. Secrecy Order. One company, E-Systems, received $1.8 billion in classified contracts in 1993 alone. Interestingly, Raytheon, the fourth largest U.S. defense contractor, which owns the Beechcraft Corporation that built the King Air A-100 that went down in the Wellstone crash, currently holds the patents. Some may find this to be a striking coincidence.

EMPS AT EVELETH

There are a number of ways an energy-directed weapon could have been used in the Wellstone crash. A small incendiary bomb may have been placed in the airplane and activated by a radio wave when the plane was near the airport or a pulse bomb could have been fired at the airplane on approach causing the electronic system to go out of control.

> *As Wellstone's plane approaches the airport, the VOR/ILS jamming equipment is activated, and a 'decoy' VOR signal is sent to the plane, thus tricking the plane's instruments [and the pilot] into believing the airport is somewhere several degrees off the true course to the runway,"* a source wrote. *"The pilot follows that signal straight into the ground. The nondescript van, full of covert electronic jamming equipment, casually leaves the area, looking just like any other TV repair truck or moving van."*

The possibility of this might be supported by the eyewitness testimony of witnesses who said that they heard an explosion and saw a flash of light. Megen Williams, who lived near the Eveleth airport, told the *St. Paul Pioneer Press* that she heard "a diving noise and then an explosion" as she prepared for work as a nurse in her home near the crash site. At first, she thought it was blasting at a nearby iron ore mine, so she didn't call authorities. Another local resident, Rodney Allen, said the plane flew right over his house. "It was so close the windows were shaking," Allen said. He added that the craft was "crabbing to the right," then less than a minute later, he felt an impact and heard what he thought sounded like a loud rifle shot *(St. Paul Pioneer Press,* October 26, 2002). A blond-haired man on CNN similarly reported that he had observed a flash of light at the rear of the plane shortly before the crash.

If the plane had been hit by such a weapon, that could explain why

Don Sipola, a former president of the Eveleth Virginia Municipal Airport Commission, has reported "something" caused Wellstone's plan to veer off course at low altitude. "This was a real steep bank, not a nice, gentle don't-spill-the-coffee descent," Sipola said. "This is more like a space shuttle coming down. This was not a controlled descent into the ground." It would also account for the cessation of communication simultaneous with cessation of control and Ongaro's odd cell phone anomaly. The use of such a weapon might also have been combined with a small bomb that was wired to the stall warning device, which would explode as the King Air A-100 came in for what was otherwise going to be a conventional landing. That might lend support to the NTSB's cover story that the plane had been subject to a very rapid descent at the time the alarm sounded, making it impossible to recover from the loss of altitude.

It is certainly far more reasonable to conclude that some form of a "directed-energy weapon", such as an electro-magnetic pulse bomb, was used to wreak havoc on the plane's electronics or otherwise destroy its functioning than to suppose that "something unexpected happened". That, after all, is no explanation. Something unexpected happened, all right: the question is, precisely what? EMPs generate an intense "blast" of electromagnetic waves in the microwave frequency band that is strong enough to overload electrical circuitry. It is like shooting lightning at a plane.

Modern airplanes use electronics rather than linkages for flight control, so EMPs can cause serious malfunctions and cause a plane to crash. EMPs now are relatively easy to obtain. Anyone can acquire an EMP generator through the internet. Thus, in principle, a person a few miles from the runway could bombard the aircraft with an intense electromagnetic pulse, which could cause an electrical failure, instantly knock out radio communication, disrupt normal engine ignition, and cause loss of steering control. The steering control surfaces on these airplanes are controlled by individual electrical actuators that are mechanically linked to the rudder, ailerons, and flaps. The loss of control would be complete.

This type of sabotage would leave no physical evidence on the aircraft, apart from an 8-day clock that would have continued to operate up until the crash. It's possible that people at the airport or in the general vicinity might have noticed electrical anomalies like radio noises, a crashed computer, telephone disruption, and so on. A Texas software engineer wrote that EMPs damage systems by generating an electrical pulse in the system wiring. Therefore, a component would not have to be directly exposed to an EMP to be damaged. An aircraft struck by an EMP pulse would not likely die in the sky, unless the plane was hit by an extremely powerful EMP pulse. "More likely, an EMP strike would disable delicate electronic systems, leaving electrical systems intact," he observed. "After being struck by an EMP, the aircraft would likely function more or less normally, but without any control systems, instruments, or radios." It might wander around in the sky in a crab-like fashion before it assumed a downward trajectory and crashed into the surrounding terrain.

This would account for the assertion that the Wellstone plane's engines were still running when the plane hit the ground. Another electrical engineer wrote that "You don't need anything as elaborate as an EMP generator. Standard issue radio transmitters can screw up a landing." Recall that the smoke from the fire was blue, not black. Jet fuel burns black. Electrical fires burn blue. The electrical systems are in the fuselage, which was burning blue. The jet fuel was located in wing tanks and the wings were separated from the fuselage. An electrical fire from an EMP bomb would explain it and, indeed, the plan might have called for redundancy, first by using some small bomb connected to the stall warning system to throw everyone into a panicked state, then hit it with an EMP weapon to make sure the plane was out of control and that communications had been severed. That would all but guarantee the outcome.

LOGIC AND EVIDENCE

Scientific reasoning is a pattern of thinking things through that proceeds through stages of puzzlement, speculation, and adaptation, ending with a (tentative and fallible) explanation. It should be applied in every context complicated and serious enough to require it, including the death of JFK and the recent death of Senator Paul Wellstone. When we apply scientific reasoning, we discover that the truth may not be what the papers print or what our government tells us. The tragedy appears to have been another political assassination. Here is an overview of how we have come to this conclusion.

Stage I: PUZZLEMENT: What brought this plane down?

Something caused this crash and it was not the plane, the pilots, or the weather. That means we have to consider other, less pleasant alternatives, such as small bombs, gas canisters, or high tech EMP (RF or HERF gun) weapons. But if we are overlooking some alternative, then even when we have eliminated the others, we may not have isolated the correct explanation. This is basic to scientific reasoning about this or any other puzzling situation. This is the stage of speculation by identifying all the possibilities.

Stage II: SPECULATION: What are the alternative possibilities?

They include a range of possible failures that are consistent with an accident, such as

(h1) mechanical problems with the plane;
(h2) difficult weather caused the crash;
(h3) the pilots made mistakes in flying;
(h4) something unexpected happened like:
> (h4a) a prop came off and hit the plane;
> (h4b) the plane hit some gaggle of geese; or
> (h4c) some unspecified alternative..., which does not entail

sabotage or other deliberate efforts to cause the plane to
crash.

Notice that, if we have overlooked one or more possible explanation under (h4c), then even if we conclude that the plane was brought down deliberately, we may have more investigative work to do, since a new alternative may require reconsidering the adequacy of our study.

But they also include a range of alternatives that are consistent with assassination, such as

(h5) something unexpected happened like:
> (h5a) a small bomb exploded in the plane;
> (h5b) some gas canister induced a stupor;
> (h5c) a ground-based weapon was employed,
>> which would be consistent with
>>> (h5ci) an EMP type weapon was employed; or
>>> (h5cii) an RF type weapon was employed,
>>> including

(h5ciii) a HERF gun; or else,

(h5civ) some other type of high tech weapon

Where the distinction between (h4) and (h5) corresponds to that between non-political (unintentional) modes of causation and political (intentional) modes of causation. Only at the level of (h5) are we confronted with death by means of assassination.

Stage III: ADAPTATION: How do the alternatives fit the evidence?

The evidence that leads us to take (h5) and its alternatives seriously includes such considerations as the following:

(h1) This particular plane was one of the most reliable of small aircraft and had an excellent maintainance history, with no serious problems; even the NTSB has cleared the plane of fault.

Infer: not-(h1).

(h2) The weather was not ideal but far from serious; planes were landing there earlier; the airport manager took off immediately when the plane did not land; photographs taken in the immediate area show no signs of serious weather; a driver in the area saw no signs of serious weather; early reports that the time were being corrected by local reporters who knew there was no "freezing rain", for example, and who were pilots themselves. That weather was a problem is highly improbable. Even the NTSB did not cite the weather.

Infer: not-(h2).

(h3) There were two qualified pilots; the primary had 5,200 hours of flight time and the highest possible certification; he has passed his flight check just two days before the fatal flight; those with the most experience flying with him described him as the most careful pilot they had ever flown with; he displayed prudence about flying on October 25, 2002 until the weather had cleared; Wellstone, who did not like to fly, was comfortable with him (implying that he was indeed a very cautious pilot); if something had happened to him, the co-pilot could have taken over; and so on. The NTSB report blamed it on the pilots.

Infer: not-(h3)

There is much additional evidence that supports the elimination of (h1), (h2), and (h3), including the NTSB's own simulations, which included pilots from Charter Aviation and which involved simulations at much reduced speeds. None of them was able to take down the plane. It is impossible to replicate exactly the pilot variables, since they are no longer with us, but there is no good reason to suppose that these simulations—which appear to be consistent with the other evidence on (h1), (h2), and (h3)—are not reliable. This means that, unless we introduce rather far-fetched alternatives, such as that both pilots wanted to commit suicide, both were under the influence of LSD, which had been put in their water, or some such, which are possible but very improbable, we accept the probable inference that neither the plane nor the weather nor the pilots appear to have been responsible. That moves us on to:

(h4) Something unexpected happened like:

(h4a) a prop came off and hit the plane, except there is no evidence of that and the NTSB investigation has cleared it, so we

Infer: not-(h4a);

(h4b) the plane hit some gaggle of geese, except that there was not remnant of any gaggle of geese, feathers, goose parts, or things like that present at the scene; so we

Infer: not-(h4b);

(h4c) some unspecified alternative..., which remains open-ended until some such alternative is specified for consideration; so we

Infer: leave (h4c) in suspense by neither accepting (h4c) nor rejecting (h4c).

Apart from supposing that something was the cause but we don't know what it was (an enigma wrapped in mystery shrouded in mist), to the extent to which we are rational in the formation of our beliefs, we are logically forced by all the above to consider other, more sinister, alternatives, which imply an assassination: (h5) something unexpected happened like: (h5a) a small bomb exploded in the plane, where, insofar as we know of no reports of shrapnel wounds to the bodies of the pilots or the passengers, especially since the passengers were badly burned; we infer: not-(h5a), while recognizing that new evidence may force reconsideration;

(h5b) some gas canister induced a stupor, an alternative Jim initially proposed, which should have left gas residues in the bodies, where no residues have been found; so we Infer: not-(h5b), again recognizing new evidence could matter here;

(h5c) a ground-based weapon was employed, which appears to us to have been the case for reasons that we have explained. The possible alternatives include: (h5ci) an EMP type weapon was employed; (h5cii) an RF type weapon was employed; including (h5ciii) a HERF gun; or else (h5ciii) some other type of high tech weapon was used....The tenability of (h5c), of course, is the current locus of debate. But notice the chain of argument that led us to this point. We are certainly not experts on RF, EMP, or HERF gun technology; and we admit that we could be wrong about this; but the rest of the available evidence appears to undermine the accident alternative, including:

(e1) the anomalous cell-phone experience of John Ongaro;

(e2) the FBI's early arrival on the scene by around noon;

(e3) the exchange of roles between the FBI and the NTSB;

(e4) the insider's report to Michael Ruppert that this had been a hit and that others were likely to follow; not to mention the general political context, which included:

(e5) that Wellstone had been targeted for political elimination by the Bush machine;

(e6) that the control of the Senate was at stake (which has made quite a difference);

(e7) that Cheney threatened him and his home state with "severe ramifications"; plus additional considerations that were more or less peculiar to this case:

(e8) the non-availability of FAA information about planes landing at Duluth International Airport on October 25, 2002, which Jim Fetzer had requested;

(e9) the cancellation of hearings the NTSB ordinarily conducts to receive public input, excused on the basis of the contention this was not a "high profile case";

(e10) a flurry of early reports that have "spun" responsibility toward the pilots, when that appears to be unjustifiable when all the evidence is taken into account.

Bear in mind, of course, that the NTSB was restricted to the consideration of only non-assassination hypotheses. The assassination alternatives were not available for its consideration and, for that reason, no doubt, were not encompassed by its investigation. We agree that, if the only three alternatives were (h1), (h2), and (h3), then even we would find (h3) to be the most likely, in spite of its very low likelihood. But, like Richard Healing, we would also be compelled to admit that we were merely speculating. We too would admit we do not know what caused this crash. And that was the case because the NTSB was taking into account only part of the available relevant evidence, in blatant violation of the scientific requirement of total evidence.

Stage IV: EXPLANATION: Which alternative should we accept?

Infer: This was no accident; the motives were almost certainly political; and the White House, or its representatives, may have been involved; where this inference is both tentative (it is subject to revision with the acquisition of further evidence or new alternatives) and fallible (even though it may be the most rational of the alternatives, it might still be false). We are dealing with inductive reasoning in accumulating evidence and in appraising its logical force. The structure of the argument incorporates deductive steps, of course, which entail the elimination of various alternatives. But it remains inductive overall, since new evidence or additional alternatives might require reconsideration of the inference that this was an assassination.

Everyone should understand that our argument goes as far as (h5c), where we are open-minded about precisely what kind of weapon may have been used. We conjecture that it might have been an EMP weapon, but we are open-minded in relation to other high tech weapons, such as a HERF gun. We have discovered that the NTSB's own conclusion is contradicted by its own evidence. This means that the likelihood that this crash was the result of an accident is approximately zero. Not only do neither (h1) nor (h2) nor (h3) account for the evidence which has been enumerated above as (e1) through (e10)—which is non-exhaustive— but none of those variations on the accident hypothesis can account for these:

(e11) the abrupt cessation of communication simultaneous with loss of control;

(e12) whatever caused the loss of control was almost certainly responsible for the concurrent cessation of communication; and,

(e13) the most likely time for this plane to have been hit is between 10:18 and 10:20, which brings us back to (e1).

According to inference to the best explanation, an alternative (hi) is preferable to an alternative (hj) when (hi) provides a better explanation of the evidence than does (hj). An alternative provides a better explanation when it confers a higher probability on the available evidence. The likelihood of an hypothesis on given evidence (e) is equal to the probability of (e), if that hypothesis were true. Having a higher likelihood makes an hypothesis preferable, but it is not also acceptable until sufficient evidence has become available. And, given the evidence enumerated above, it does appear to have "settled down," which means that the hypothesis with the highest likelihood ought to be accepted.

We have already shown that the likelihood that the death of Paul Wellstone was an accident approaches zero as its value, given what we know about the plane, the weather, and the pilots. Given the NTSB's own simulations, moreover, it cannot be sustained. Not only is the accident hypothesis undermined by the NTSB's evidence but it cannot account for (e1) through (e13) above. The probability of evidence of kind (e1) through (e13), given the assassination hypothesis, by comparison, is very high. The relative likelihoods of the accident hypothesis (approximately zero) and the assassination hypothesis (very high) mean that the assassination hypothesis is reasonable, while the accident hypothesis is not. This also means that we have proven scientifically that the death of Senator Paul Wellstone was an assassination.

We are not so naive as to think that proving the assassination hypothesis beyond a reasonable doubt means that most Americans are going to accept our conclusion. The principles of social psychology and the manipulation of the mass media by the government as an exercise is propaganda makes that a virtual impossibility. But we are heartened that others have taken the same evidence and have arrived at similar conclusions. Gradually, as more and more citizens begin to think things through, we believe that they will recognize that no alternative to the assassination hypothesis is remotely reasonable and that the evidence places the assassination hypothesis beyond reasonable doubt.

HIGH TECH WEAPONS IN THE MEDIA

The existence of high tech weapons of the kind that were apparently employed to bring down the Wellstone plane is gradually becoming more familiar to the public. Beyond articles like the one in *Time* we cited above, the *Arizona Daily Star* (April 8, 2004), explains that Raytheon has a new non-lethal electromagnetic weapon system for disabling enemy soldiers or hostile crowds with a painful beam of energy. The devices can be mounted on military vehicles for rapid deployment. And *Boston Business Journal* (August 5, 2004) has reported that a new "directed energy" weapon Raytheon has developed "that makes one's skin feel as though it is on fire" should be in the possession of the U.S. military "by the end of the year."

Other recent developments include reports about malfunctioning keyless vehicle entry devices by the *Las Vegas Review-Journal* (February 21, 2004), where more than a hundred drivers complained about the mysterious failure of their remote opening mechanisms to work, which was highly probably a consequence of electromagnetic weapons operating in the area at the time. A local physician reportedly learned that several patients from the Eveleth-Virginia area had an experience that had puzzled them: Their automatic garage doors had opened spontaneously that day, about the time of the crash.

Other students of the crash have arrived at conclusions that are very similar to those presented in this book. In response to the suggestion of a critic that the Wellstone pilots had misjudged their altitude and airspeed, much as the NTSB would conclude, Kelly Duke offered the following response with a new hypothesis:

> Yes, planes do "fall out of the sky" occasionally, but there is almost always SOME tenable explanation for these accidents. In this case, This is the critical occurrence that no one (including the NTSB) who has argued that the crash was due to pilot error has ever addressed. How did the plane somehow drift or turn well over a mile off course—a huge navigational error over

a period of at least 90 seconds—during its final instrument approach? The standard and safest King Air procedure for a VOR IFR (instrument flight rules) approach is to use the autopilot to steer the plane toward the VOR beacon (see "Non-precision approach" at www.navfltsm.addr.com/vor-appr.htm). Note that (even though asserting this much already obviously strains credulity to impossible levels), it's not enough to simply posit that both Conry and Guess managed to ignore the fact that the CDI needle was pegged all the way to the left for over 90 seconds while they somehow managed not to notice that they had slowed more than 60 mph below the recommended approach speed until the stall warning horn was blaring in their ears at which time they made the cardinal sin of attempting too sharp of a power turn at too low of an altitude. This "explanation"—such at it is—entirely begs the question of how the King Air A-100's autopilot, an extremely reliable piece of equipment that another pilot confirmed was functioning normally just the day before, managed to steer the plane so far off course. If we assume that the crash was accidental, the only possibilities are:

(A) The pilots decided the make the approach manually AND while attempting this less safe manual approach, neither pilot ever even glanced in the direction of the CDI needle, which would have been their only directional guidance in overcast conditions (all while mysteriously and fatally slowing almost to stall speed, of course). In addition, note that the NTSB summary of interviews (www.startribune.com/style/news/politics/wellstone/ntsb/252886.pdf) states, "When Conroy flew, he would always fly with the autopilot engaged."

(B) The pilots somehow managed to engage the autopilot on the wrong target. But in this case another question is begged—namely, what other possible target could have given them a remotely reasonable DME (Distance Measuring Equipment) reading? But this option—like so much about this crash—argues for foul play. (For example, go to news.xinhuanet.com/english/2003-01/14/content_688638.htm.) Of course, if we don't assume this crash was accidental, then we can choose from a myriad of reasonable explanations for this otherwise unexplainable chain of events. Here is just one that I find entirely plausible:

(1) A "service vehicle" equipped with both a decoy VOR beacon with a stronger signal than Eveleth Airport's VOR and an Active Denial System weapon (go to—boston.bizjournals.com/boston/stories/2004/08/02/daily40.html) is placed 1-2 miles south of the airport, probably off road, and nearly the same distance from the final VOR approach turn as the airport's actual VOR beacon (so that the DME would read as expected just after to the final approach turn).

(2) After the plane finishes its final approach orientation and the Duluth ATC signs off, the overriding VOR signal is switched on. Note that Eveleth Airport is seldom used, and that any pilots further than 30 miles away who were using Eveleth's VOR for navigation purposes (if there were any) wouldn't even notice the tiny change in needle (and perhaps course) deflection that homing in the the new overriding target would entail. Further note the "on again/off again" cover story about Eveleth's VOR being "slightly out of tolerance" just in case somebody DID notice any temporary problem or discrepancy in navigation (news.minnesota.publicradio.org/features/2003/03/03_zdechlikm_wellstone/).

(3) In the cloudy, overcast conditions, Wellstone's pilots would be basically relying on autopilot to guide the plane horizontally to the VOR—in this case the false, overriding decoy VOR—resulting in the plane being drawn off course in the exact manner the radar returns demonstrate.

(4) When the plane is drawn off course close enough to get in the range of the ADS weapon (currently classified but almost certainly 1/2 a mile), the cockpit area is zapped—resulting in an effectively pilotless plane. Of course, many other weapons could have been used, but this one has the expository advantage of recently appearing in several high profile, mainstream news stories.

(5) The overriding decoy VOR is then switched off, causing the

plane's instruments to reorient to Eveleth Airport's real VOR. This last minute reorientation would cause the still engaged autopilot to attempt a sharp right turn—"crabbing to the right," in the words of one eyewitness—exacerbating the loss of control of the already pilotlessplane (www.twincities.com/mld/pioneerpress/4376969.htm

(6) After the plane crashes, someone would presumably make sure the cockpit instruments were consumed in flames—just on the remote chance that a serious, full inquiry were to be demanded—as the "cable TV/power company/telephone service vehicle" makes its escape from the scene of the crime.

Kelly Duke is not the only one to suggest this to us. Bradley Ayers, an experienced investigator, also stated that messing with the VOR may have been an important component in bringing about the crash. We are not ruling out this hypothesis. The evidence suggests that the primary cause of the crash, however, was the cessation of communication and control by one or another in a new family of high-tech weapons of the EMP variety. But it is possible that the VOR could have been simulated, as Duke proposes, or even manipulated, as Ayers believes, to bring the aircraft into the vicinity of vulnerability from such a device. Physical manipulation might even have left it a few degrees out of alignment, which was the NTSB's own finding. So we find these possibilities as extremely plausible.

Some may find the fact that Raytheon not only owns Beechcraft, which makes the King Air A-100, but also manufactures high tech weapons of the kind that were used to bring it down, where Raytheon representatives were on the crash scene during the on site investigation, more than a striking coincidence. Anyone who has studied the deaths of prominent politicians, such as President Kennedy and Senators Carnahan and Wellstone, has to give pause to the prospect that the military industrial complex has been flexing its muscle in promoting political policies and administrations that are sympathetic to their corporate interests. Although we are not accusing Raytheon of having had a role in this assassination, some may find this inference a difficult one to resist. And there is certainly enough evidence here to consider the possibility that Raytheon provides the link between the Bush administration and the Wellstone crash.

Proof of assassination is not proof of conspiracy. But the use of a high-tech weapon strongly suggests that Wellstone's death also entailed a conspiracy. The political motives for taking him out, more-over, offer reasons to conjecture that Karl Rove, Dick Cheney, and Donald Rumsfeld—the troika that actually runs the Bush administration—are the most likely to have been involved. Recent revelations about Cheney's obsession with going to war in Iraq, the probability that he was responsible for disclosing the identity of Ambassador Wilson's CIA undercover wife, and his threats to Senator Wellstone have impressed us as the actions of a powerful, unscrupulous zealot. We believe that a formal investigation of the Wellstone case should begin with Vice President Cheney.

Our website warrior enemies have assumed that we plan to bring legal action against the Bush administration for the death of Senator Wellstone. We have been accused of not being able to satisfy the necessary requirements for a legal prosecution of Cheney, Rove, and Rumsfeld as responsible for the death of Senator Paul Wellstone. But that is not what we are about. We are trying to figure out the causes of the crash, which would be essential before any consideration is given to its legal ramifications.

CHARACTER ASSASSINATION

Another form of assassination is to trivialize, belittle, or otherwise tarnish a man's reputation, even after his death. Shortly after his death, the "Sentry Over America" website posted an editorial (in its issue 21) entitled, "Why Mourn For Paul Wellstone?" It describe this as, "Just another enemy death. Paul Wellstone was an enemy soldier in the army of Socialist Democrats who have reigned terror and destruction on the U.S. Constitution and all those beliefs that we cherish. Our men in uniform in Afghanistan do not mourn the loss of dead Taliban. I do not mourn the loss of Paul Wellstone." Marianne M. Jennings, who is a professor of legal and ethical studies at Arizona State University, expressed similar sentiments in an article published in *Jewish World Review* on November 4, 2002:

> *I don't buy the ethos or nobility of Wellstone or other 60's remnants who*

*rely on factless emotion and flawed reasoning. Wellstone had perfected the
liberal methodology for notoriety, regard, and invincibility, even from
Republican opponents.*

Claims of "factless emotion" and "flawed reasoning", of course,
require evidence to substantiate them, since otherwise they
themselves qualify for those descriptions.

Continuing her attack, she cited a speech made by Wellstone
in August 1999, opposing welfare reform. She implied that he
tried to evoke sympathies for four children living with their
grandmother and relying on federal breakfast and lunch
programs. She said that Wellstone "taunted Republicans for
starving this family" but that, "for a man just canonized in St.
Paul, he was a bit loose with truth" because he failed to disclose
that the mother of the four children was a crack addict and
that the grandmother a recovering addict who "paid cash for a
two pack a day cigarette habit." It can be a fine line to
distinguish between legitimate debate over political values and
attempts to tarnish the reputation of the dead, but comments
like these, which were published close to the time of the
Senator's death, may exemplify a trend.

They display the same abuse of logic and mean-spirit that charac-
terize the influential right-wing "hate radio" host, Rush Limbaugh.
Limbaugh's success was orchestrated and initially sponsored by
Republican powers. His television show debuted nationally just two
months before the 1992 election. His producer, Roger Ailes, was also
Bush's media advisor throughout the campaign. Many of the themes
Ailes used earlier in the campaign showed up in virtually
identical forms on Rush's show, which approximated program-length
commercials for the Bush campaign. (See Don Trent Jacobs, *The
Bum's Rush* (1994)).

Could it be that individuals were being encouraged to start
attacks on Wellstone before he became a martyr? The National
Rifle Association has used similar tactics by giving strong pro-
gun speeches in communities where school shootings have just
occurred to discourage the spread of anti-gun sentiment. And
it has been a common tactic in regime change politics where
there is a risk that the outgoing leader's loyal sympathizers
might not support the new leadership. We take for granted that

the NRA and other special interest organizations are going to spread false information. But the threat of disinformation emanating from universities, however, strikes an entirely different chord. If the very idea that a university professor might be hired or otherwise coaxed into publishing propaganda for the government sounds just too paranoid or just plain smacks of a "conspiratorial whacko," then consider this quote from the 1976 Select Committee to Study Governmental Operations with Respect to Intelligence Activities, which was chaired by the then Idaho Senator, Frank Church:

> *The Central Intelligence Agency is now using several hundred American academics (where that term includes administrators, faculty members and graduate students engaged in teaching,) who in addition to providing leads and, on occasion, making introductions for intelligence purposes, occasionally write books and other material to be used for propaganda purposes. Beyond these, an additional few score are used in an unwitting manner for minor activities.*
>
> *These academics are located in over 100 American colleges, universities, and related institutes. At the majority of institutions, no one other than the individual concerned is aware of the CIA link. At the others, at least one university official is aware of the operational use made of academics on his campus. The CIA considers these operational relationships within the U.S. academic community as perhaps its most sensitive domestic area and has strict controls governing these operations. (See The Final Report of the "Church Committee", published on April 26, 1976)*

We are not asserting that Jennings or the writer for "Sentry Over America" are hired guns for those who eliminated Wellstone. At the street level of political opinion, it's been assumed on both the Left and the Right that Wellstone's political enemies took him out. Any liberal commentators out there who are afraid to look at our conclusion, perhaps should take a lesson from voices on the Right, who are basking in it. In these times of the Patriot Act and the other new levels of disinformation and propaganda, we confront a greater and ever growing need for the exercise of critical thinking just to understand what's going on.

We have demonstrated that the official account of the

strange death of Senator Paul Wellstone cannot be sustained. The hypothesis that the crash was an accident has a likelihood of approximately zero, given the available relevant evidence, while the hypothesis that the crash was an assassination has a likelihood that is high. A conclusion has been established beyond a reasonable doubt when no alternative explanation is reasonable. We have proven that no alternative to the assassination hypothesis is reasonable. If we are right in our belief—where we have elaborated our reasons for thinking so in considerable detail—then we have proven the assassination hypothesis beyond a reasonable doubt.

The death of Paul Wellstone, as tragic as it may be, assumes even greater significance in relation to its place in an apparent pattern of governmental misconduct to preserve and protect this and other corrupt administrations. If we don't understand what this means, our feeble grasp on democracy will be lost, possibly forever. There are lessons here that every American must learn for the sake of our country and of the principles for which it is supposed to stand and for which, alas, an American icon died.

EPILOGUE

strange (adj)

1. of another place or locality; foreign; alien
2. not previously know, seen, heard, or experienced; unfamiliar
3. quite unusual or uncommon; extraordinary
4. queer; peculiar; odd
5. reserved, distant, or cold in manner
6. lacking experience; unaccustomed

—*Webster's New World Dictionary* (1988)

We live in "strange" times, in every sense of the word. The United States, once a model for freedom, has become an aggressor nation. We violate international laws. We abrogate treaties, and even our own constitutional precepts, just as we did with the American Indian nations. Once the most admired country in the world, The United States is among the most reviled. (In the UK, a February 2003 Channel 4 poll found that Britons believe the US is the #1 threat to international peace.) We seem to have forgotten, as Jack Kennedy observed, "our most basic common link is that we all inhabit this small planet. We all breathe the same air. We all cherish our children's future. And we are all mortal."

The Republican Party used to stand for balanced budgets, constitutional government, a non-interventionist foreign policy, and keeping government out of people's personal lives. It has taken a 180° turn. The GOP has adopted a neo-conservative, empire-building agenda. Its corporatizing priorities owe loyalty to nothing but short-term profits. The exploitation of cheap labor occurs in off-shore deals that evade US taxes. The GOP has embraced the values of fundamentalist Christian zealots, who believe the government should dominate the most private decisions of our personal lives. We live in a country that would have been unimaginable to the Founding

Fathers.

It's essential to understand what happened after JFK was assassinated. The same techniques of deception, alteration, fabrication, and manipulation operate today just as they did on and after November 22, 1963. Nowhere is this more apparent than in the deceptions surrounding 9/11. American citizens lag behind the rest of the world in understanding that day. The truth has been obfuscated by the American government, and the national media is complicit. A growing number of people are learning that our "war president" and his Administration went to great lengths to stonewall the official investigation of 9/11. Bush nominated Henry Kissinger to chair the panel. (Kissinger can not travel in some countries due to warrants out for his arrest for international war crimes.) Although Kissinger's conflicts of interest made this impossible, it ultimately didn't matter. The 9/11 Commission's final report was itself a whitewash.

The death of Senator Paul Wellstone, like that of JFK, represents a tragedy of monumental proportions. Both events redefined the "the American way of life". In lieu of a government of, by, and for the people, we have a government of, by, and for multinational corporations. To some, "fascism" is too strong a word to describe our present government. But Benito Mussolini observed that "fascism" could be simply defined as "corporatism", since it is the merger of big business with big government.

In fascism, the leader is identified with the state, so that any criticism of the leader is viewed as unpatriotic or even treasonous. The emergence of the grossly misnamed "U.S.A. P.A.T.R.I.O.T. Act" leave little doubt that fascism is on the rise. Donald Rumsfeld envisions the U.S.A.'s "Full Spectrum Domination" of our planet and outer-space. His side sees this as the natural future new world order, unconstrained by constitutional government or by international law.

A growing movement would like to see the United States resurrect its past commitments to freedom and democracy at home and abroad. Senator Paul Wellstone was among them. The American people must come to grips with the underlying reality of fascism, American-style. Like fascism in other forms, it relies upon selective assassination, and, in its more virulent form, systematic genocide.

Perhaps the greatest challenge to this book will be the American reluctance to believe the worst about ourselves—that those in control of our government might kill its elected officials. Even knowing that political assassinations have occurred throughout history, we cannot imagine that our great country could fall prey to similar corruptions. As we pointed out earlier, even those who do not believe that JFK was assassinated by pro-war policy makers because they think JFK was more or less alligned with that policy, must now know that Senator Wellstone stood strongly against the Bush-Cheney agenda. A similar anti-JFK assassination conspiracy argument would have no substance at all.

Ultimately, we hope this book will awaken the American people from our devolution into fascism. We hope this awakening will happen before a Nazi-like regime makes assassinations a part of normal policy. Let us learn from the inspiring example of Paul Wellstone provided by taking steps to set things right. Until *we the people* regain political ascendancy in the United States, *we the people* must brace ourselves for more wars and assassinations.

PAUL WELLSTONE:
WHAT HE STOOD FOR

PART ONE

THE PLATFORM OF
SENATOR PAUL WELLSTONE

One of the 50 Most Effective Members of Congress"
—*Congressional Quarterly*

• Proposed putting two billion dollars into Minnesota's schools instead of further tax cuts for the top 1% of incomes.

• Saved consumers hundreds of millions by stopping last-minute back-door efforts by drug companies to extend their exclusive patents.

• Said no to privatizing social security.

• Teamed up with Republicans and got things done for Minnesotans on worker training, mental health parity, domestic violence, Parkinson's research, anti-sex trafficking, and training teachers.

• Helped strengthen and pass the McCain-Feingold campaign finance reform bill, and passed laws banning gifts to members of Congress and better regulating lobbyists.

• Passed a strong, Minnesota-friendly farm bill with Wellstone-written amendments that reduced the advantages of corporate agribusiness and moved the focus back to family farms.

• Twice led the fight to stop Big Oil from drilling in the Arctic National Wildlife Refuge.

• A champion on veterans' issues, he recently wrote and passed the Homeless Veterans Assistance Act.

• Taking on the insurance industry lobby to pass a strong

Patients' Bill of Rights and a decent prescription drug benefit.

AMERICAN INDIAN SOVEREIGNTY

Member of the United States Senate Indian Affairs Committee, Senator Wellstone has served on the Senate Indian Affairs Committee since 1991. This committee deals with issues such as Indian education, economic development, land management, trust responsibilities, health care, and claims against the federal government.

Senator Wellstone has been a strong ally of American Indian people. He supports treaty rights and tribal sovereignty and has worked to promote and strengthen healthy tribal governments. Wellstone believes that tribes must have the right to self-determination in order to continue their successful policies of economic development. With sovereignty, tribal governments have been able to implement policies on Minnesota reservations that have created jobs in areas of high unemployment and generated revenues that have been invested back into the community

In 2000, Senator Wellstone enacted legislation that authorized the Lower Sioux Community to sell non-trust lands without getting Congressional approval for each specific sale.

FEDERAL EDUCATION FUNDING BEFORE ADDITIONAL TAX BREAKS FOR THE WEALTHY.

Paul is fighting to put $2 billion over ten years into Minnesota's schools, where it belongs. Paul knows that educating Minnesota's kids should come before tax breaks for large multi-national corporations and the wealthiest 1% of taxpayers (people making more than $300,000 a year). The clear choice is to eliminate planned tax breaks for the wealthy and put that money into education. This increased funding would allow local schools to hire additional teachers, reduce class-size, modernize public buildings, buy more books and computers, early childhood education and increase parental involvement.

PROVIDING FUNDING TO HIRE TEACHERS, SCHOOL CONSTRUCTION, AND AFTER-SCHOOL PROGRAMS.

Paul voted for a legislative amendment that would have authorized funding for specific educational purposes, including hiring new teachers, building and repairing schools, and running after school programs.

INCREASING FUNDING FOR CLASS-SIZE REDUCTION.

Paul voted for an amendment that would have required $1.4 billion to be spent on the class-size reduction program; it would add an extra $350 million that would have to be spent on that program.

100,000 NEW TEACHERS SHOULD BE HIRED TO REDUCE CLASS SIZE.

Paul voted in favor of an amendment stating, "Congress should support efforts to hire 100,000 new teachers to reduce class sizes in first, second, and third grades to an average of 18 students per class all across America."

RECRUITING, RETAINING, AND TRAINING TEACHERS.

Working in conjunction with conservative Republican Kay Bailey Hutchison of Texas, Paul introduced a measure that provides $250 million in grants and scholarships to recruit and train teachers in high-need districts. It was passed by the Senate as part of the Education Reform Bill of 2001.

PROVIDING TEACHER INCENTIVES FOR WELL-PERFORMING SCHOOLS.

Paul voted for an amendment allowing Teacher Empowerment Act funds to be used to implement programs that: reward teachers in schools with improvement in student achievement, help teachers acquire advanced degrees in the subjects they teach, implement rigorous peer review, evaluation, and recertification programs, and provide incentives for highly qualified teachers to teach in needy schools.

INCREASING FUNDING FOR SPECIAL EDUCATION.

Paul cosponsored a measure that provided full funding for

special education. The measure was added to the Education Reform Bill in the Senate last year but was ultimately knocked out of the final bill by the Republican White House and Republican House Leadership.

WORKING TO PROVIDE BILLIONS FOR SPECIAL EDUCATION PROGRAMS.

Paul Wellstone fought to put $2 billion over ten years into Minnesota's schools in special education funding, thereby fulfilling Congress' commitment. Educating Minnesota's kids should come before tax breaks for large multi-national corporations and the wealthiest 1% of taxpayers. Increased funding would allow local schools to hire additional teachers, reduce class-size, modernize public buildings, purchase more books and computers, improve early childhood education and increase parental involvement. Paul also passed a tri-partisan amendment through the Senate to fully fund IDEA, the Individuals with Disabilities Education Act. This amendment was stripped out in conference with the Republican House of Representatives. [S. Amdt. 360 to S. 1, 107th Congress, 3 May 2001]

SUPPORTED MEASURES PROVIDING $2 BILLION FOR DISABILITY PROGRAMS.

Wellstone voted in favor of a measure to provide $2 billion over 5 years to finance disability programs that allow persons with a disability to become employed and remain independent. [Vote #282, Motion Rejected 47-51, 105th Congress, 2nd Session, 2 April 1998]

FIGHTING TO REMOVE RESTRICTIONS ON DISABILITY PAYMENTS.

Wellstone cosponsored a measure that would remove the federal income-eligibility limits for Americans with disabilities who receive federal benefits, thus allowing more disabled citizens to work without being penalized. It passed through the Senate by a 99-0 margin in 1999.

EXPANDED HEALTH CARE SERVICES

FOR DISABLED WORKERS.

Wellstone voted in favor of the Ticket to Work and Work Incentives Improvement Act, which expanded the availability of health care services for Americans with disabilities in the workforce and created the Ticket to Work and Self Sufficiency Program, giving beneficiaries access to employment services, vocational rehabilitation services, and other support services from employment networks of their choice. [Vote #372, Conference Report Agreed To 95-1, 106th Congress, 1st Session, 19 November 1999]

IMPROVED FLEXIBILITY OF FEDERAL PROGRAMS.

In 1998, Paul Wellstone and Senator DeWine (R-OH) introduced and passed the Workforce Investment Act. The act reorganized multiple federal job training, adult education and vocational rehabilitation programs into a few broad streams of funding while giving state and local governments more flexibility in designing and implementing their training programs. [Wellstone Release, 31 July 1998; Vote #119, Bill Passed 91-7, 105th Congress, 2nd Session]

**EXPANDED HEALTH CARE SERVICES
FOR DISABLED CHILDREN.**

Paul Wellstone voted to allow disabled children of legal immigrants to receive Medicaid benefits. [Vote #118, Motion Rejected 49-51, 105th Congress, 1st Session, 25 June 1997]

SENATE AGRICULTURE COMMITTEE

Paul Wellstone is a member of the Senate Agriculture Committee, a key Congressional committee with broad oversight over all agriculture, nutrition, and forestry issues facing America.

REFORM OF AMERICA'S FARM POLICY.

Paul Wellstone voted against the Freedom to Farm Act—legislation that has hurt family farmers and rewarded corporate farmers and farm interests over the last few years. Speaking at a Rally for Rural America in March 2000, Wellstone called for strong anti-trust action against corporate farms. He also has advocated raising the loan rate to give farmers more leverage in the marketplace, and boost farmer incomes while promoting conservation practices.

PROVIDING DISASTER RELIEF FOR FARMERS.

Paul Wellstone has helped secure millions in disaster relief funding for Minnesota farmers who have been hurt by floods and low commodity prices.

WELLSTONE SUPPORTED THE FARMER-OWNED RESERVE PROGRAM.

Paul Wellstone supported an amendment to the Freedom to Farm Bill of 1996 by Sen. Harkin that would have reinstated the Farmer-Owned Reserve Program, which paid farmers 26.5 cents per bushel to store grain instead of selling it.

WELLSTONE WROTE, PROMOTED AND PASSED THE VEGETABLE INK LAW.

Paul Wellstone wrote, promoted, and passed legislation that is now the law of the land making the government increase its use of vegetable-based ink—such as soy ink—in nearly all its printing operations.

WELLSTONE PROPOSED AGRICULTURE RELIEF PLAN FOR NORTHWEST MINNESOTA'S FAMILY FARMERS.

In March 1998, Paul Wellstone announced a package of agriculture relief measures he was introducing to relieve economic pain in Minnesota's Red River Valley farming region. He joined Rep. Collin Peterson and others in proposing changes to federal crop insurance, including adjusting crop histories to avoid penalizing farmers for disaster years and increasing planting flexibility and access to insurance coverage.

WELLSTONE SUPPORTED DAIRY ASSISTANCE DUE TO LOW MILK PRICES.

Paul Wellstone supported $473 million in direct income relief payments contained in the FY '01 Agriculture Appropriations that would go to dairy farmers throughout the nation. Based on past distribution methods, the average eligible Minnesota farmer would receive about $6,000.

WELLSTONE INTRODUCED A MEASURE
TO REPEAL THE NORTHEAST DAIRY COMPACT.

In April 1999, Paul Wellstone introduced legislation to repeal the Northeast Dairy Compact, an unfair, artificial pricing scheme that has brought economic hardship to Minnesota's dairy producers.

WELLSTONE OPPOSES THE PORK CHECK-OFF;
SUPPORTS ENDING THE TAX ON PORK FARMERS.

Paul Wellstone adamantly opposes the "pork-check off" tax on family hog farmers and supports the results of a referendum by family hog farmers to end the check-off. President Bush's Agriculture Department has sided with the National Pork Producers Council—a trade association—in opposing the results of the referendum and supporting large corporate hog farms over the interests of family hog farmers. The check-off is an assessment of 45 cents for every $100 in hog sales

WELLSTONE INTRODUCED A MEASURE TO PROVIDE A
SAFETY NET FOR FARMERS.

Paul Wellstone introduced legislation in January 2001 to protect struggling family farmers by making permanent Chapter 12 provisions in the U.S. Bankruptcy Code. Chapter 12 of the Bankruptcy Code is an important safety net for family farmers, providing critical protection for them when they find   themselves   in desperate economic circumstances.

WELLSTONE SUPPORTED MEASURES TO HELP ENSURE
FAIR PRICES FOR LIVESTOCK PRODUCERS.

Paul Wellstone supported funding for the Grain Inspection, Packers and Stockyard Administration (GIPSA) in FY '01. The allocation contained $31.42 million in funding to help ensure competitive markets and fair prices for America's livestock producers.

WELLSTONE VOTED IN FAVOR OF THE SUGAR PROGRAM.

Paul Wellstone voted in favor of tabling an amendment to

the FY '01 Agriculture Appropriations bill that would have prohibited using funds from the appropriations bill to pay the salaries and expenses of Agriculture Department personnel to carry out the Federal sugar program.

WELLSTONE SPONSORED THE MEASURE EXPRESSING SENSE OF CONGRESS THAT PARTICIPANTS IN 'RALLY FOR RURAL AMERICA' ARE COMMENDED.

Paul Wellstone sponsored and voted in favor of an amendment to the Risk Management for the 21st Century Act that expressed the sense of the Congress that 'the participants in the Rally for Rural America [March 20-21, 2000] are commended' and that Congress should respond to rural America in a way that will 'alleviate the agriculture price crisis; ensure competitive markets; invest in rural education and health care; protect our natural resources for future generals; and ensure a safe and secure food supply for all.'

WELLSTONE SUPPORTED A $30 BILLION RESERVE FUND FOR FARMERS.

Paul Wellstone supported an amendment to the Concurrent Budget Resolution for Fiscal Years 2000-2009 that would replace the bill's $6 billion reserve fund for farmers with one totaling $30 billion.

RESPONSE TO ECONOMIC HARDSHIP FACING FARMERS.

Paul Wellstone voted in favor of an amendment to the FY '99 Agriculture Appropriations bill by Sen. Daschle that expressed the sense of the Senate that immediate action by the President and Congress is necessary to respond to the economic hardships facing agricultural producers and their communities.'

WELLSTONE SUPPORTED OUTLAWING MTBE FUEL.

Paul Wellstone supported a measure that would express the sense of the Senate that MTBE fuel should be outlawed. Wellstone favors biomass-derived fuel additives such as ethanol to MTBE.

WELLSTONE SUPPORTED THE ETHANOL TAX CREDIT.

Paul Wellstone voted to block a measure that would have allowed the tax credit for ethanol fuel to expire after the year 2000.

WELLSTONE COSPONSORED THE FARMERS AND RANCHERS COMPETITION ACT TO RESTORE COMPETITION IN AGRICULTURE.

In April 2000, Paul Wellstone joined Senators Tom Daschle and Patrick Leahy in introducing sweeping legislation today to combat anti-competitive practices by agribusinesses that have proven harmful to family farmers and ranchers in Minnesota and across the nation. The legislation, The Farmers and Ranchers Fair Competition Act, came in response to growing concentration in the agriculture sector of America's economy. It would have made unlawful unfair practices in transactions involving agriculture commodities, established a pre-merger review within the USDA to ensure proposed mergers do not hurt family farmers, establish a commission to provide compensation for injuries involving unfair practices, and required disclosure standards for production and marketing contracts. "Dairy farmers are in the midst of a crisis," Wellstone said. "My state of Minnesota lost over 600 dairies last year alone. Concentration has increased among processors and grocers alike, and family farmers have been almost completely squeezed out."

WELLSTONE SPONSORED MEASURE PLACING A MORATORIUM ON MERGERS OR ACQUISITIONS INVOLVING AGRIBUSINESS.

Paul Wellstone sponsored and voted in favor of an amendment to the Bankruptcy Reform Act of 1999 that would have placed a moratorium on mergers or acquisitions involving agribusinesses in which one business had annual net revenue or assets of more than $100 million and the other business had annual net revenue or assets of more than $10 million. The moratorium would have lasted for 18 months or until legislation was passed to limit concentration in agriculture markets. Farmer cooperatives would be exempt from the moratorium.

JOBS, SMALL BUSINESS, & CONSUMER PROTECTION

WELLSTONE WORKED TO CUT RED-TAPE, CHANGING THE OPPRESSIVELY SLOW FEDERAL REVIEW OF MEDICAL DEVICES.

Wellstone's reforms cut review times while protecting consumer safety. Since the reforms became law, medical technology firms have thrived in Minnesota.

HELPING TECHNOLOGY COMPANIES ACCESS MINNESOTA'S RURAL WORKFORCE

Working with small businesses across Minnesota, Wellstone wrote the Rural Telework Act of 2000, and passed it as part of the 2002 Farm Bill. This Act increases opportunities for technology based businesses to locate and expand in rural areas. Expanding Broadband Access to Every Corner of the State as part of the recently passed farm bill, Wellstone supported grants to rural communities to expand access to broadband technology that encourages job growth.

JOB TRAINING & RELIEF

Wellstone introduced the "Wellstone Workforce Recovery" bill to provide tax breaks for working families, an extension of unemployment insurance, health care benefits for laid-off workers, $2 billion in new job training programs, additional funding for child care, and relief for small businesses.

"GROWING" MINNESOTA JOBS WITH STRONG INCENTIVES FOR BIO-FUELS

Paul Wellstone's tireless work to support renewable bio-fuels like corn ethanol and soy-based bio-diesel has produced jobs in Minnesota's rural communities. The incredible growth in Minnesota's bio-fuel industry is a victory for Minnesota's farmers, the economy and the environment.

HELPING SMALL BUSINESSES ACCESS CAPITAL

On the Small Business Committee, Paul Wellstone has focused on expanding access to capital for small businesses.

Wellstone has championed micro-loan programs that provide capital to very small start-up businesses that are often denied other loan options.

WELLSTONE STRENGTHENED MCCAIN-FEINGOLD BY CLOSING A MAJOR LOOPHOLE.

The Wellstone amendment bans special interest groups from running ads against a candidate for public office within 60 days of the general election or 30 days of a primary election. It passed the U.S. Senate 51-46.

WELLSTONE STOOD UP FOR AMERICAN JOBS AND THE ENVIRONMENT AND OPPOSED NAFTA.

Citing the anticipated loss of American jobs and the lack of environmental protections in the agreement, Paul Wellstone opposed the North American Free Trade Agreement.

WELLSTONE STOOD UP FOR FAIR TRADE AND OPPOSED THE PASSAGE OF GATT/WTO.

Paul Wellstone opposed the General Agreement on Tariffs and Trade. The trade accord created the World Trade Organization and allows it to undercut U.S. sovereignty by allowing panels of foreign judges to rule on whether federal and state laws constitute impermissible impediments to trade.

WELLSTONE FOUGHT FOR MEASURES TO PROMOTE FAIR TRADE

The Senator supported bills and amendments that:

- Required that trade benefits be provided in accordance with a country's compliance with internationally-recognized labor standards

- Denied trade benefits to countries which failed to meet child labor standards

- Prohibited the selling of dumped or subsidized merchandise if it threatened U.S. industry

- Ensured that corporations and countries respect the rights of employees, the environment, and American workers

- Prohibited food or medicines from being a part of economic sanctions on a foreign country

- Exempted farm exports from trade sanctions

WELLSTONE OPPOSED FAST-TRACK TRADING AUTHORITY.

Paul Wellstone opposed renewing Fast-Track trade negotiating authority that provides no meaningful protections for workers, the environment, and our right to pass and maintain laws in the public interest, and that cedes to the executive branch powers reserved to Congress by the Constitution.

WELLSTONE WORKED FOR TRADE RELIEF FOR AMERICAN STEEL INDUSTRY.

Paul Wellstone worked with other Senators and Representatives from both parties to get fair trade protections for the U.S. steel industry and its workers.

Wellstone helped convince President Bush to continue a Clinton administration investigation into U.S. imports of iron ore and steel.

Wellstone signed a bipartisan letter with more than a dozen senators in March 2001 asking President Bush for trade relief on behalf of the American steel industry.

Working with Senator Mark Dayton, Paul Wellstone introduced the Steel Revitalization Act of 2001 to make more loans available to American steel companies and set restrictions on the imports of iron ore, semifinished steel and finished steel products.

Senators Wellstone and Dayton introduced the Taconite Workers Relief Act of 2001, to ensure that the taconite industry benefits fully from U.S. trade laws and that taconite workers qualify for trade assistance benefits if they lose their jobs because of foreign trade.[Taconite is a low-grade iron ore. Once considered just a pesky rock, it's in demand now since the earth's supply of high-grade natural iron ore is low.]

WELLSTONE VOTED AGAINST PERMANENT NORMAL TRADE RELATIONS WITH CHINA.

Paul Wellstone voted against final passage of the United States-China Relations Act of 2000, which allowed the President to grant the People's Republic of China (PRC) permanent normal trade relations status with the United States. He supported numerous amendments to the bill that would have helped establish a fair trade relationship with China rather than an unfettered free trade relationship. They would have required:

- Presidential certification that China was complying with prohibition of the importation and exportation of prison labor products

- Presidential certification that China was meeting human rights conditions and respect for religious freedom before granting permanent normal trade relations

- A business code of conduct for businesses with investments in China

- The monitoring of China's environmental practices

- The monitoring of U.S.-China trade relations

- The elimination of the $60 billion per year trade deficit with China

- Protections to U.S. businesses against market-disrupting surges of imports from China

FIGHTING TO EXPAND
OPPORTUNITIES FOR WOMEN

Paul Wellstone has been a leader in the U.S. Senate on behalf of women across Minnesota and the rest of America. Wellstone co-authored the Violence Against Women's Act and pushed to expand and reauthorize that act. Wellstone cosponsored the Family and Medical Leave Act of 1993 and has pushed for additional family and medical leave in the workplace. Wellstone has also been a leader when it comes to women's health care, pushing for assistance to women in the fight against breast and cervical cancer.

WELLSTONE COAUTHORED THE VIOLENCE AGAINST WOMEN'S ACT; URGED THE REAUTHORIZATION AND EXPANSION OF THE ACT.

Paul Wellstone led the effort to reauthorize and expand the Violence Against Women Act (VAWA). Wellstone was an original cosponsor of the original 1994 Violence Against Women Act, which established the first-ever penalties for violence against women. In 2000, Wellstone pushed for the passage of the Violence Against Women Act (VAWA) II, an expansion of the original law intended to provide additional funding for initiatives to prevent domestic violence and protect victims with violence at home. VAWA II provides more resources to combat domestic violence for police, prosecutors, victim services, courts, shelters, rape prevention efforts, and initiatives that address the economic consequences of violence in the lives of women.

WELLSTONE COSPONSORED THE FAMILY AND MEDICAL LEAVE ACT OF 1993.

Paul Wellstone voted in favor the Family and Medical Leave Act of 1993, which allowed employees to take time with their family without losing their job.

WELLSTONE FOUGHT FOR AN EXPANSION OF FAMILY AND MEDICAL LEAVE ACT.

Paul Wellstone fought to expand the Family and Medical Leave Act so that more of Minnesota's working families could take advantage of this type of leave. Wellstone's measure would have provided workers with short-term job security in times of family or medical emergencies. If a person needed time off to care for a new child, or to care for a sick child, spouse, or elderly parent, the person's job and health insurance would be secure. Wellstone also sponsored a measure that would allow Family and Medical Leave time to address domestic violence and its effects.

WELLSTONE COSPONSORED THE FAIR PAY ACT OF 2001.

Paul Wellstone cosponsored the Fair Pay Act of 2001, a measure to amend the Fair Labor Standards Act of 1938 to prohibit discrimination in the payment of wages on account of sex, race, or national origin.

WELLSTONE COSPONSORED AN EQUAL RIGHTS AMENDMENT TO THE U.S. CONSTITUTION.

Paul Wellstone long supported the idea of passing an Equal Rights Amendment to the United States Constitution and cosponsored the measure in the 107th Congress.

WELLSTONE SUPPORTED A WOMAN'S RIGHT TO CHOOSE 100% OF THE TIME.

Paul Wellstone was always a strong supporter of a woman's right to choose both in and out of the U.S. Senate.

WELLSTONE VOTED IN FAVOR OF MEASURE PROVIDING UNLIMITED COMPENSATORY AND PUNITIVE DAMAGE AWARDS IN GENDER DISCRIMINATION LAWSUITS.

Paul Wellstone voted in favor of a measure by Sens. Harkin and Daschle that would have amended the Fair Labor Standards Act to permit unlimited compensatory and punitive damages to be awarded in gender discrimination lawsuits regarding pay rates (including in class-action lawsuits), and would increase the burden on employers to prove that any pay rate differentials between jobs primarily held by men and jobs primarily held by women were based on bona fide factors, such as education or experience. The amendment would also require the Labor Department to educate employers on the requirements of the law.

WELLSTONE FOUGHT TO REPEAL THE CAP ON DAMAGES AVAILABLE TO WOMEN WHO ARE VICTIMS OF SEXUAL HARASSMENT.

Paul Wellstone supported and fought for a measure to repeal a cap on damages available to women who are victims of sexual harassment. The measure was an amendment to the 1991 Civil Rights Act.

WELLSTONE PUSHED FOR HEALTH CARE COVERAGE FOR BREAST CANCER VICTIMS.

Paul Wellstone cosponsored legislation that required health insurance companies provide coverage for a minimal hospital stay for mastectomies and lymph node dissection for the treatment of breast cancer and coverage for secondary consultations.

WELLSTONE PUSHED FOR BREAST & CERVICAL CANCER ASSISTANCE.

Paul Wellstone cosponsored a Senate measure that provided medical assistance for certain women who have been screened and found to have breast cancer or cervical cancer under a federally   funded   screening program.

WELLSTONE COSPONSORED MEASURE TO PROVIDE WOMEN HEALTH CARE ACCESS TO OBSTETRIC AND GYNECOLOGICAL SERVICES.

Paul Wellstone cosponsored a Senate measure to require health insurance plans to provide women with adequate access to   providers   of   obstetric   and gynecological services.

WELLSTONE VOTED FOR INCREASED PATIENT PROTECTIONS FOR BREAST CANCER AND OBSTETRICAL/GYNECOLOGICAL PATIENTS AND SELF-EMPLOYED HEALTH CARE TAX DEDUCTIONS.

Paul Wellstone voted in favor of an amendment to the Patient's Bill of Rights Act that would have imposed mandates on the length of hospitalization after breast cancer surgery, and imposed mandates on obstetrical/gynecological care (all health insurance plans would be required to provide hospital care after any mastectomy, lumpectomy, or lymph node dissection for as long as the attending physician and patient thought such care was "medically appropriate" and such care was "consistent with generally accepted medical standards). The amendment would have also made the health insurance costs of self-employed Americans fully deductible (the cost of that tax benefit would be paid for over 5 years not by cutting other spending out of the $1.7 trillion Federal budget but by increasing Superfund (environmental waste cleanup) taxes by $6.7 billion).

WELLSTONE VOTED IN FAVOR OF A MEASURE ALLOWING PROCEEDS FROM SPECIAL STAMP TO GO TOWARDS BREAST CANCER RESEARCH.

Paul Wellstone voted in favor of an amendment to the Treasury-Postal Service FY '98 Appropriations by Senator Feinstein that gave people the option of purchasing first-class postage stamps that cost 1 cent more than other first-class stamps. The 1-cent differential, after subtracting Postal Service expenses, would be given to the Department of Health and Human Services for breast cancer research.

WELLSTONE SUPPORTED INCREASING FUNDING FOR BREAST CANCER SCREENING BY $50 MILLION.

Paul Wellstone voted in favor of a measure by Senator Harkin that would have increased appropriations for breast cancer screening by $50 million.

Wellstone Petitioned President Clinton to put together a "Comprehensive Plan to End the Breast Cancer Epidemic." Paul Wellstone marched with thousands of breast cancer activists and survivors to the White House in October 1993 to petition President Clinton to 'bring together leaders from his administration, the Congress, the scientific community, private industry and women to support this plan.

WELLSTONE:
WHAT HE STOOD FOR

PART TWO

PAUL WELLSTONE
"ON IRAQ"

October 3rd, 2002
On Iraq
Statements by Senator Paul Wellstone to the U.S. Senate

I rise to address our policy in Iraq. The situation remains fluid. Administration officials are engaged in negotiations at the United Nations over what approach we ought to take with our allies to disarm the brutal and dictatorial Iraqi regime.

The debate we will have in the Senate today and in the days to follow is critical because the administration seeks our authorization now for military action, including possibly unprecedented, preemptive, go-it-alone military action in Iraq, even as it seeks to garner support from our allies on a new U.N. disarmament resolution.

Let me be clear: Saddam Hussein is a brutal, ruthless dictator who has repressed his own people, attacked his neighbors, and he remains an international outlaw. The world would be a much better place if he were gone and the regime in Iraq were changed. That is why the United States should unite the world against Saddam and not allow him to unite forces against us.

A go-it-alone approach, allowing a ground invasion of Iraq without the support of other countries, could give Saddam exactly that chance. A preemptive, go-it-alone strategy toward

Iraq is wrong. I oppose it. I support ridding Iraq of weapons of mass destruction through unfettered U.N. inspections which would begin as soon as possible. Only a broad coalition of nations, united to disarm Saddam, while preserving our war on terror, is likely to succeed.

Our primary focus now must be on Iraq's verifiable disarmament of weapons of mass destruction. This will help maintain international support and could even eventually result in Saddam's loss of power. Of course, I would welcome this, along with most of our allies.

The President has helped to direct intense new multilateral pressure on Saddam Hussein to allow U.N. and International Atomic Energy Agency weapons inspectors back in Iraq to conduct their assessment of Iraq's chemical, biological, and nuclear programs. He clearly has felt that heat. It suggests what can be accomplished through collective action.

I am not naive about this process. Much work lies ahead. But we cannot dismiss out of hand Saddam's late and reluctant commitment to comply with U.N. disarmament arrangements or the agreement struck Tuesday to begin to implement them.

We should use the gathering international resolve to collectively confront this regime by building on these efforts.

This debate must include all Americans because our decisions finally must have the informed consent of the American people who will be asked to bear the cost, in blood and treasure, of our decisions.

When the lives of sons and daughters of average Americans could be risked and lost, their voices must be heard in the Congress before we make decisions about military action. Right now, despite a desire to support our President, I believe many Americans still have profound questions about the wisdom of relying too heavily on a preemptive go-it-alone military approach. Acting now, on our own, might be a sign of our power. Acting sensibly, and in a measured way, in concert with our allies, with bipartisan congressional support, would be a sign of our strength.

It would also be a sign of the wisdom of our Founders who lodged in the President the power to command U.S. Armed

Forces, and in Congress the power to make war, ensuring a balance of powers between coequal branches of Government. Our Constitution lodges the power to weigh the causes of war and the ability to declare war in Congress precisely to ensure that the American people and those who represent them will be consulted before military action is taken.

The Senate has a grave duty to insist on a full debate that examines for all Americans the full range of options before us and weighs those options, together with their risks and costs. Such a debate should be energized by the real spirit of September 11, a debate which places a priority not on unanimity but on the unity of a people determined to force-fully confront and defeat terrorism and to defend our values.

I have supported internationally-sanctioned coalition mili-tary action in Bosnia, in Kosovo, in Serbia, and in Afghanistan. Even so, in recent weeks, I and others—including major Republican policymakers, such as former Bush National Security Adviser Brent Scowcroft; former Bush Secretary of State James Baker; my colleague on the Senate Foreign Relations Committee, Senator Chuck Hagel; Bush Mid-East envoy General Anthony Zinni; and other leading U.S. military leaders—have raised serious questions about the approach the administration is taking on Iraq.

There have been questions raised about the nature and urgency of Iraq's threat and our response to that threat: What is the best course of action that the United States could take to address this threat? What are the economic, political, and national security consequences of a possible U.S. or allied invasion of Iraq?

There have been questions raised about the consequences of our actions abroad, including its effect on the continuing war on terrorism, our ongoing efforts to stabilize and rebuild Afghanistan, and efforts to calm the intensifying Middle East crisis, especially the Israeli-Palestinian conflict.

There have been questions raised about the consequences of our actions here at home. Of gravest concern, obviously, are the questions raised about the possible loss of life that could result from our actions. The United States could post tens of thousands of troops in Iraq and, in so doing, risk countless lives of soldiers and innocent Iraqis.

There are other questions about the impact of an attack in relation to our economy. The United States could face soaring oil prices and could spend billions both on a war and a years-long effort to stabilize Iraq after an invasion. The resolution that will be before the Senate explicitly authorizes a go-it-alone approach. I believe an international approach is essential. In my view, our policy should have four key elements.

First and foremost, the United States must work with our allies to deal with Iraq. We should not go it alone, or virtually alone, with a preemptive ground invasion. Most critically, acting alone could jeopardize our top national priority, the continuing war on terror. I believe it would be a mistake to vote for a resolution that authorizes a preemptive ground invasion. The intense cooperation of other nations in relation to matters that deal with intelligence sharing, security, political and economic cooperation, law enforcement, and financial surveillance, and other areas is crucial to this fight, and this is what is critical for our country to be able to wage its war effectively with our allies. Over the past year, this cooperation has been the most successful weapon against terrorist networks. That—not attacking Iraq —should be the main focus of our efforts in the war on terror.

As I think about what a go-it-alone strategy would mean in terms of the consequences in South Asia and the Near East and the need for our country to have access on the ground, and cooperation of the community, and get intelligence in the war against al-Qaida and in this war against terrorism, I believe a go-it-alone approach could undercut that effort. That is why I believe our effort should be international.

We have succeeded in destroying some al-Qaida forces, but many operatives have scattered. Their will to kill Americans is still strong. The United States has relied heavily on alliances with nearly 100 countries in a coalition against terror for critical intelligence to protect Americans from possible future attacks. Acting with the support of allies, including, hopefully, Arab and Muslim allies, would limit possible damage to that coalition and our antiterrorism effort. But as General Wes Clark, former Supreme Commander of Allied Forces in Europe, has recently noted, a premature, go-it-alone invasion of Iraq "would supercharge recruiting for al-Qaida."

Second, our efforts should have a goal of disarming Saddam Hussein of all his weapons of mass destruction. Iraq agreed to destroy its weapons of mass destruction at the end of the Persian Gulf War and to verification by the U.N. and the International Atomic Energy Agency that this had been done. According to the U.N. and the IAEA, and undisputed by the administration, inspections during the 1990s neutralized a substantial portion of Iraq's weapons of mass destruction, and getting inspectors back to finish the job is critical. We know he did not cooperate with all of the inspection regime.

We know what needs to be done. But the fact is we had that regime, and it is important now to call on the Security Council of the U.N. to insist that those inspectors be on the ground. The goal is disarmament, unfettered access. It is an international effort, and with that Saddam Hussein must comply. Otherwise, there will be consequences, including appropriate use of force. The prompt resumption of inspections and disarmament, under an expedited timetable and with unfettered access in Iraq, is imperative. Third, weapons inspections should be enforceable. If efforts by the U.N. weapons inspectors are tried and fail, a range of potential U.N. sanctions means, including proportionate military force, should be considered. I have no doubt that this Congress would act swiftly to authorize force in such circumstances. This does not mean giving the United Nations a veto over U.S. actions. Nobody wants to do that. It simply means, as Chairman Levin has observed, that Saddam Hussein is a world problem and should be addressed in the world arena.

Finally, our approach toward Iraq must be consistent with international law and the framework of collective security developed over the last 50 years or more. It should be sanctioned by the Security Council under the U.N. charter, to which we are a party and by which we are legally bound. Only a broad coalition of nations, united to disarm Saddam

Hussein, while preserving our war on terror, can succeed. Our response will be far more effective if Saddam Hussein sees the whole world arrayed against him. We should act forcefully, resolutely, sensibly, with our allies—and not alone—to disarm Saddam Hussein. Authorizing the preemptive go-alone use of force right now, which is what the resolution before us calls for, in the midst of continuing efforts to enlist the world community to back a tough, new disarmament resolution on Iraq, could be a very costly mistake for our country.

"I do not believe the future will belong to those who are content with the present. I do not believe the future will belong to those who are cynics or to those who stand on the sidelines. The future will belong to those who have passion and to those who are willing to make a personal commitment to make our country better."

—Senator Paul Wellstone

ABOUT THE AUTHORS

FOUR ARROWS
(AKA DONALD TRENT JACOBS)

Four Arrows holds a Ph.D. in health psychology and an Ed.D. in curriculum and instruction. Former Dean of Education at Oglala Lakota College and a former Marine Corps officer of the Vietnam Era, he is an associate professor in the Department of Educational Leadership at Northern Arizona University and a faculty member at the College of Educational Leadership and Change at Fielding Graduate Institute. His most recent books include: *Indigenous World Views: First Nations Scholars Challenge Anti-Indian Hegemony; Teaching Virtues* (2001), *Primal Awareness* (1997), and *The Bum's Rush* (1994). President of the Northern Arizona Chapter of Veterans for Peace, he has been a vocal critic of U.S. foreign policy. Dr. Jacobs recently received the Martin-Springer Institute's 2004 Moral Courage Award.

PRAISE FOR FOUR ARROWS' TEACHING VIRTUES:

"This splendid book brings to education one of the most neglected and abused resources of our continent: the deep knowing of American Indian people. This is precisely what we need to revitalize our educational systems. Everyone who reads this book with an open heart and mind will emerge wise and stronger."
—Parker Palmer, *The Courage to Teach*

"I read this book with great interest, for the topics addressed are of great importance for educational practice, and hence, for the larger society. They approach the issues of character education from a variety of directions, including a highly suggestive American Indian perspective that has been far too little understood in our culture. This book is a stimulating and thoughtful contribution to character education."
—Noam Chomsky, MIT

PRAISE FOR THE BUM'S RUSH:

"Refreshing and biting."
—Michael W. Apple
  John Bascom Professor of Educational Policy Studies,
  University of Wisconsin, Madison

"At this critical moment in history, when so many people are struggling to live responsibly in relation to the Earth, this book will help honest individuals understand and counter the bullying tactics of Rush Limbaugh and his handlers."
—Steve Richardson,
  Executive Director, Environmental Action Coalition

PRAISE FOR PRIMAL AWARENESS:

"As I turned its pages, I was moved to laughter and tears. I highly recommend it to anyone interested in the mysteries of the human mind and heart."
—Dan Millman, author of Way of the Peaceful Warrior and Everyday Enlightenment

"I can say without reservation that Primal Awareness will help make the world a better place if enough people read it."
—Edwin Bustillos
  Winner of Goldman Environmental Award (Survivor of
four assassination attempts by the Fontes Drug Cartel)

JIM FETZER

McKnight Professor of Philosophy at the University of Minnesota, Duluth, has published extensively in the philosophy of science. Also a former Marine Corps officer of the Vietnam Era, he has edited three books on the death of JFK: *Assassination Science* (1998), *Murder in Dealey Plaza* (2000), and *The Great Zapruder Film Hoax* (2003). He maintains a web site devoted to this and related subjects at *www.assassinationscience.com*.

PRAISE FOR ASSASSINATION SCIENCE:

"Assassination Science is a watershed....the cool clinical breeze of rigorous thinking blows throughout."
    —Kerry Walters, Ph.D.,
    Distinguished Professor, Gettysburg College

"Every serious student of the Kennedy assassination should read this excellent compilation of articles, which dissect and destroy The *Warren Commission Report* in a meticulous, objective, and analytical manner."
    —Cyril Wecht, M.D., J.D.
    Coroner, Allegheny County
    Past President, American Academy of Forensic Sciences

"The accumulation of carefully researched detail will impress those with an open mind. Fetzer, a professor of philosophy at the University of Minnesota, takes the position that thorough and disinterested scientific research cannot but conclude that more than one assassin was involved....The discussion of the Zapruder film is especially noteworthy..."
    —*Publishers Weekly*